The Legacy of Américo Paredes

NUMBER TEN:
Rio Grande/Río Bravo
Borderlands Culture and Traditions
Norma E. Cantú, *General Editor*

The Legacy of AMÉRICO PAREDES

JOSÉ R. LÓPEZ MORÍN

Texas A&M University Press
College Station

FIRST EDITION

The paper used in this book meets the minimum requirements
of the American National Standard for Permanence
of Paper for Printed Library Materials, Z39.48–1984.
Binding materials have been chosen for durability.

An earlier version of chapter 2 was presented at the 2001
"Folklore on the Border: The Legacy of Américo Paredes"
conference at UCLA and later appeared in the spring 2005
issue of *Western Folklore*.

Library of Congress Cataloging-in-Publication Data

Lopez Morín, José R.
The legacy of Américo Paredes / José R. López Morín.
p. cm. — (Rio Grande/Rio Bravo ; no. 10)
Includes bibliographical references and index.
ISBN-13: 978-1-58544-509-7 (alk. paper)
ISBN-10: 1-58544-509-6 (alk. paper)
ISBN-13: 978-1-58544-536-3 (pbk. : alk. paper)
ISBN-10: 1-58544-536-3 (pbk. : alk. paper)
1. Paredes, Américo. 2. Mexican American authors—Texas—Biography.
3. Authors, American—20th century—Biography. 4. Folklorists—
United States—Biography. 5. Paredes, Américo. With his pistol in his hand.
I. Title. II. Series.
PS3531.A525Z75 2006
813′.54—dc22
2006001563

Para mis padres,
Segundo López de la Fuente,
un aficionado
de los corridos
y sus intérpretes
favoritos
Los Alegres de Terán;
y para mi madre,
María Odilia Morín de López,
por su sentido de humor,
sonrisa,
y gran sacrificio
siempre
para que sus hijos
salieran
adelante.
Este libro es para ustedes,
con todo el amor
del mundo.

Contents

List of Illustrations / ix
Preface / xi
Acknowledgments / xvii

Chapter 1:
The Lower Rio Grande Border / *1*

Chapter 2:
His Life and Work / *33*

Chapter 3:
"With His Pistol in His Hand" / *70*

Chapter 4:
Toward New Perspectives in Folklore and Cultural Anthropology / *97*

Conclusion / 127
Notes / 133
Works of Américo Paredes / 149
Bibliography / 157
Index / 167

Illustrations

Gallery of photographs follows page 69.

Américo's parents, ca. 1914

Américo with his sister Blanca, ca. 1920

Américo at Camp Robinson, Arkansas, 1945

Américo practicing guitar, Brownsville, Texas, early 1930s

Américo in Tokyo, Japan, 1946

Amelia Shidzu Nagamine and Américo Paredes in Tokyo, 1948

Américo celebrating his thirty-third birthday in Tokyo

Paredes with a radio presenter from station XEO, 1958

As a professor at the University of Texas at Austin, 1970s

Américo Paredes in his late seventies

Preface

"With His Pistol in His Hand": A Border Ballad and Its Hero (1958), Américo Paredes's most-acclaimed work, generated a considerable amount of interest and enthusiasm during the rise of the Chicano movement. The text provided young activists with a convincing literary document of Mexican American resistance against U.S. hegemony. The book narrates the life and legend of Gregorio Cortez, a man who defended his rights with his pistol in his hand. The point of view presented by Paredes challenged stereotypes of Mexican Americans, since for too many years the U.S. literary record had offered an often-distorted view of Mexican culture. In general terms the mestizo people in the United States were viewed as inferior and backward with no serious desire to better themselves or their lot. Paredes rejected this attitude in much of his writings throughout his entire career at the University of Texas at Austin. He believed that Mexican American folklore and culture in general was limited in scope and often inaccurate in its attempts to understand the people.

A variable within his revisionist efforts was his idea of folklore as "performance." The concept involved a shift of emphasis away from the collection and origin of cultural items and into an examination of folklore as a *communicative process* and with the genius of the folk artist in mind. Rather than being the object of representation, folklore as performance served as a voice for Paredes to understand what it meant to be a Mexican in the United States. The spin allowed for another point of view, one that was seldom considered by folklorists and cultural anthropologists. Writing about culture in this way foreshadowed an important trend many years later known as the postmodern movement in the social sciences. My argument in this book attempts to prove that Paredes's contribution to the study of culture not only establishes him as a one of the most influential folklorists of his time, but also as an important figure in cultural anthropology. Paredes was well versed in the latest cultural theories and methods of his time when he challenged the representation of Mexicans and Chicanos in his article "On Ethnographic Work among Minority Groups: A Folklorist's Perspective" (1977). The essay points toward some of the inaccuracies of cultural anthropologists who studied Mexican and Chicano communities, while his recommendations for the study of culture represent a groundbreaking text in the field of the social sciences. His techniques in ethnography and knowledge of folklore as performance show that he was ahead of his time and that the discipline of cultural anthropology would profit from a serious consideration of his contribution.

Américo Paredes was a curious and meticulous individual, who at an early age loved to read and write and who dreamed about one day becoming a famous poet and novelist. After high school graduation (1934), he attended and graduated from Brownsville Junior College (1934–36) and worked as a proofreader for the *Brownsville Herald*. He wrote poetry, short stories, and essays on Chicano culture, although a good portion of this early material remained unpublished for years. His dedication to the written word went hand in hand with his love of music, especially the piano and guitar. Américo Paredes was born into a culture that celebrated life through music, and ballads served as a form of oral history for the Mexican people. Américo sang and played guitar on the radio in his youth and became an accomplished folk singer along the Lower Rio Grande Border. He married the well-known singer Consuelo "Chelo" Silva, and the couple had a son, Américo Paredes Jr. But the marriage did not last, and Américo and Consuelo soon divorced. He later volunteered to serve in World War II and became editor of the army newspaper *Pacific Stars and Stripes* (1945–46). While in Japan he met and married his second wife, Amelia Shidzu Nagamine, daughter of a Japanese diplomat to Argentina. Amelia would be instrumental in his life and career as a professor and scholar of Chicano studies. She assumed most of the family responsibilities to allow her husband to continue his dream of one day becoming a famous writer.

The Paredes family arrived in the United States in 1950, and Américo enrolled immediately as a full-time student at the University of Texas at Austin. At home, Amelia assumed most of the household chores and the care of their first newborn, Alan, while her husband managed a full load of courses every semester. The difficult schedule allowed Paredes to complete his bachelor's degree in English and philosophy in one year (1951), summa cum laude. Later as a graduate student, he worked as a teaching assistant and instructor in English and completed his master's degree in 1953 followed by a Ph.D. in 1956. Both degrees were in English (folklore) and Spanish. His dissertation, "El Corrido de Gregorio Cortez: A Ballad of Border Conflict," was a study of one Texas Mexican *corrido* (folk song) in its cultural and historical context. After a year at the University of Texas–El Paso, the University of Texas at Austin hired him in 1957; he was forty-two. Before his death on May 5, 1999, at the age of eighty-three, Américo Paredes received many awards and distinctions and influenced a generation of scholars in folklore, anthropology, and ethnomusicology. His presence and scholarship transformed the University of Texas at Austin, establishing it as one of the most prestigious universities in the country in folklore research and interdisciplinary studies.

This book is intended for readers who know very little about Américo Paredes and wish to learn about his life and his contributions to anthropology, folklore, history, literature, and music.

It will appeal to those teaching undergraduate and introductory graduate courses in Chicano/Latino literature, southwest history, folklore, and culture more generally. Although many scholars have written extensively on Paredes's life and scholarship, I felt the need to make his work as accessible as possible because there is much to be learned from Américo Paredes. His name appears in acknowledgments, dedications, introductions, songs, anthologies, newspapers, and academic journals, and a middle school has been named for him. With this book I hope to further honor his name.

It was not easy to pinpoint or frame Américo Paredes's narrative. His intellectual curiosity and cross-disciplinary perspective made it difficult to categorize his work, and in no way do I propose to completely define it. My objective is to offer an introduction to his life and scholarship while highlighting what some critics have said about his book *"With His Pistol in His Hand."* Paredes's prose is poetic, academic, ethnographic, ironic, in Spanish and English, yet it is always accessible. His in-between sensibility, moreover, allowed him to reflect on and represent in his fictional and scholarly work the Mexican American experience with a unique double vision. This *frontera* awareness led him to formulate a sense of Chicano identity and culture that involved the use of "performance" or "role-playing" to resist the oppressive forces and negative stereotypes caused by the clash between the Mexican and North American cultures. To play the fool or the "dumb" Mexican became a sort of weapon for the border folk, and Américo Paredes was well aware of this mischievous behavior. Few critics have studied this topic thoroughly in his writings.

And for those who admire his scholarship and know his work well, I trust there will be new ideas within this book for future investigation. I also hope that I am not accused of attempting to duplicate Américo Paredes's prose, something that is quite difficult to do. But after reading and rereading his work for so many years, it became a part of my own writing style in the process of research and critique. More importantly, I hope that scholars will forgive me if they recognize certain ideas as being unmistakably theirs. Let there be no doubt that I have been influenced by their writings and their insight has contributed to the shaping of my own ideas with reference to Américo Paredes's life and scholarship.

Chapter 1, "The Lower Rio Grande Border," sets the stage for understanding the history and people of south Texas. It offers the background of the first settlers into the area, their contact with the indigenous people, and the blending of cultures that evolved from a Mexican ranching economy. North American expansionism disrupted this way of life when Texas separated from Mexico and was later annexed by the United States. Culture conflict characterizes the differences between the two groups since each group understood life and land in their own way. Many North Americans thought the Mexican people were lazy and inferior, and they expressed these opinions quite openly in their literature. But the attitudes of the first Mexican Americans toward the new settlers were rarely acknowledged in written works as it was not a part of their tradition. These experiences were remembered through oral tradition and were at the core of Américo Paredes's formation.

Chapter 2, "His Life and Work," is about Américo Paredes. He was a bright and good-natured individual who was immersed in the functional aspects of southwest culture. What becomes evident in his youth is his preoccupation with and search for answers to a life between two worlds, one that was learned orally at home and the other through the written word in school. In an effort to be heard and understood Américo wrote poetry, short stories, a novel, and he sang and played guitar. His narrative titled *George Washington Gómez: A Mexicotexan Novel* (1990) presents his early fictional examples of folklore as performance. The ability to mock people in certain situations is a special talent that was used by the poets of the border, and Américo Paredes was sensitive to this sort of activity. He knew that joking with others was a part of an oral tradition that very few outsiders understood and that verbal artists were quick to spot a pigeon when they saw one. These tongue-in-cheek commentaries became a form of entertainment for the people along the Lower Rio Grande region.

Chapter 3, "With His Pistol in His Hand," focuses on his most famous work, in which he merged a Mexican oral legacy with a Protestant Anglo-Saxon literary tradition. Here, Américo Paredes offered a distinct Chicano point of view to challenge the conventional interpretations of Mexican Americans. The conflict of cultures is at the center of Américo Paredes's argument, in which he demonstrates that where there is power, there is resistance. Chapter 3 also includes a discussion of what some critics have said about "*With His Pistol in His Hand*" and a look at Román's behavior during the horse trade with an outsider. The section closes with a brief examination of the motion picture *The Ballad of Gregorio Cortez* (1984).

Chapter 4, "Toward New Perspectives in Folklore and Cultural Anthropology," considers in more detail Paredes's performance-oriented approach, a theory that became a central theme of reference in his writings and one that combined his literary, musical, and anthropological interests to reinterpret the Mexican American people and culture. His selected essays explore the reality of Chicano culture from a variety of perspectives, and his seminal work, "On Ethnographic Work among Minority Groups: A Folklorist's Perspective," anticipated a trend in the postmodernist critique in cultural anthropology. I hold that it was Américo Paredes's unique situation between Mexico and the United States, between the social sciences and the humanities, between that of a scholar and folk performer that allowed him to revolutionize the study of culture.

Acknowledgments

Many people provided encouragement and assistance with this book, too many to list here in the acknowledgments. But special thanks are due to the following people. To Américo Paredes, who in spite of his age and failing health allowed me to interview him in the summer of 1996 to complement my library research. His generosity, sense of humor, and support I will always remember. To the Paredes family, my thanks for the photographs and permission to use them in the book. To Sergio Garza for his patience during the first stages of my research and writing, I am very grateful. To the members of my dissertation committee, Raymund A. Paredes, Efraín Kristal, Shirley Arora, Rafael Pérez-Torres, José R. Reyna, and Randal Johnson, for their guidance and encouragement with the preparation of my manuscript. A special thank you is extended to Toni M. Crowe, Robin Fisher, and the Graduate Division at UCLA for their assistance with a dissertation-year fellowship in 1998–99. This project is a reflection of their minimizing my distractions and teaching obligations. To my students at California State University, Domínguez Hills, for their support and inspiration, especially Lisette Arredondo, Rodrigo Valles, Cynthia Aldana, and Jason Hecht. My appreciation to Jerry D. Moore, professor of anthropology at CSUDH, for his reading of my final chapter and for his encouragement.

To my father, Segundo López, for sharing with me his stories about life along the Lower Rio Grande region; to my mother, Odilia M. López, who reminded me quite often to complete the book; to Frederick Luis Aldama, Richard Bauman, Sandy Crooms, John McDowell, Severo Pérez, and John M. Schechter for their consideration with e-mail responses and recommendations; to the people in Austin, Texas, especially to Margo Gutiérrez, Bill Hardesty, Michael Hironymous, Ann Lozano, Mónica Rivera, and Craig Schroer at the Nettie Lee Benson Collection Library; to José E. Limón and Frances Terry for sharing their time to assist me with my project, thank you so much; to Abel Amaya for the moments he shared with me about the times he spent with Américo at academic conferences; to Marcos Loya for his time, patience, and guidance in teaching me how to play the guitar and to perform Mexican folk songs in front of an audience; to Michael Chen for saving and transferring my notes, data, and bibliography from my old, malfunctioning computer; to Olga Nájera-Ramírez for her valuable suggestions and encouragement with the overall manuscript; to Anne R. Gibbons for her careful reading and editing of the manuscript. And to Dalia Iñiguez for her patience *y por los ánimos* during the pressures that go into the investigation, writing, and rewriting of an "almost" completed manuscript. *Muchísimas gracias a todos*.

The Legacy of Américo Paredes

Chapter 1

The Lower Rio Grande Border

The truth seems to be that the old war propaganda concerning the Alamo, Goliad, and Mier later provided a convenient justification for outrages committed on the Border by Texans of certain types, so convenient an excuse that it was artificially prolonged for almost a century. And had the Alamo, Goliad, and Mier not existed, they would have been invented, as indeed they seem to have been in part.
—Américo Paredes, "*With His Pistol in His Hand*"

When the forty-year-old Américo Paredes was writing his dissertation, which would become the basis of his best-known book, "*With His Pistol in His Hand*": *A Border Ballad and Its Hero* (1958), he drew on memories of his youth. He was especially mindful of those quiet "summer nights, in the days when there was a chaparral," when his father and the old men sat around and talked in "low, gentle voices about violent things."[1] These stories, especially the performances of *corridos*, were never forgotten by Américo Paredes. They nurtured his imagination as a young boy and became the subject of some of his most important research in his adult life.

Among the rich family oral history were tales of the arrival from Spain of his father's clan, a colony of *sefarditas* (Spanish Jews), in 1580; heroic exploits such as the participation of his great-grandfather at Palo Alto against Gen. Zachary Taylor's troops in the Battle of La Resaca; and other bitter recollections of the abuses by the Texas Rangers against the Lower Rio Grande border folk. These stories fascinated Américo as a child, and they inspired a large corpus of his writings. The heroic events of popular song and legend offered him a different picture of historical events than the formal history he learned in school. For centuries Paredes's ancestors had celebrated life through music and related events through the spoken word. Oral tradition represented the collective memory of his people, and ballads of heroic events, legends of fabulous treasures, and tales of supernatural apparitions were all an integral part of the cultural forces that shaped Mexican life. Face-to-face interaction was more important to the people than the written word, and the presence of a singer or storyteller was everyday practice. Folk poets would often recall an experience (either their own or that of others) and narrate a story with that particular idea in mind. In the process the folk poets—engrossed in the re-creation of the event—made the experience come to life for the people.

Américo Paredes's Concept of Folklore as Performance

Today, this interaction between the storyteller, audience, and the context in which a story is told is understood as the "performance-oriented" approach in folklore studies.[2] But Américo Paredes was writing before such a concept was articulated and appreciated in the field. Early folklore in general consisted of collecting songs, legends, and tales without serious consideration of the people that provided such information. Too much emphasis was given to the origin of a tale, how it traveled, or the different versions that existed in a specific region. But Américo Paredes thought differently. He felt that in order to arrive at a more reliable reading of folklore and to fully appreciate its meaning, the material needed to be studied and understood within its natural context and with the folk artist in mind. For Paredes, folklore was not divorced from daily life—something to be observed and preserved in its essence. He considered this expressive art—first and foremost—as the performance of songs, legends, and tales in keeping with the oral legacy of the Lower Rio Grande region. His take on folklore as performance emphasized the functional aspects of this expressive behavior, which, in turn, shed new light on the experiences of Mexicans in the United States.

One of Paredes's main contentions in his long life as a scholar was that North American literature had long presented a distorted view of the history of his region and people. He knew that English policy toward the Indians in the New World was different from that of the Spanish settlers. The first group traveled overseas with their families and belongings for political and religious freedom, and the Indians had no place in the creation of the new English society. The Spaniards, on the other hand, set sail to convert the native population to Christianity and to extend the power of the Spanish Empire into the Americas. Eventually, the two contrasting cultures would meet in the New World, and nowhere was their conflict as enduring as in the heart of the old Spanish province of Nuevo Santander. At the core of Américo Paredes's concerns was the cultural legacy of the conflict along the Lower Rio Grande border. His research on the corrido was the starting point and the touchstone of his contribution of a people whose children and grandchildren would identify themselves as Mexican Americans, Chicanos and Chicanas. Paredes argued in his thesis that *el corrido de Gregorio Cortez* served as a resistance literature against North

American domination. The ballad of Gregorio Cortez challenged both the stereotypical views of Mexicans and the official versions of events in the history of the border. Paredes did not write his book from the perspective of a dispassionate bystander. He felt a moral responsibility to contribute to the cultural survival of his people. As the Mexico-Tejano scholar embarked on a career at the University of Texas at Austin, he made it a lifelong quest to celebrate the spirit, wisdom, and dignity of his people.

El Nuevo Reino de León and Nuevo Santander

Américo Paredes spoke candidly about his Jewish lineage. He traced his ancestry in the Lower Rio Grande region as far back as 1580, learning by heart many of the stories his elders related to him about his ancestors, a clan of sefarditas. They were supposedly converted Spanish Jews, but many of them still kept their religious ideas in one way or another. The group was led by Luis de Carvajal y de la Cueva, a Portuguese of *converso* (Christian convert from Judaism) ancestry, who was appointed governor of el Nuevo Reino de León. Carvajal received a charter in 1579 (one of the largest of its time) that embraced the contemporary Mexican states of Nuevo León, Tamaulipas, Coahuila, almost all of Zacatecas and Durango, parts of San Luis Potosí, Nayarit, Sinaloa, Chihuahua, and Texas.[3] The grant allowed him to take one hundred people of his choice from the Iberian Peninsula to the New World and gave the new governor the privilege of passing on his holdings to his son or another heir of his own choosing. The most fascinating aspect of the charter was that all of Carvajal's passengers were excluded from the mandatory investigation of their family origins—an issue of great importance at the time, considering the discriminatory legislation then in effect against new Christians, Jews, and Muslims.[4] Even though Carvajal was of Jewish ancestry, he had given himself completely to the Catholic religion long before his appointment as governor and departure for the New World. Many of his family and friends, however, especially his wife, Doña Guiomar, were practicing Jews.[5]

Luis de Carvajal y de la Cueva was to pacify the Indians of the vast region and insure obedience to the Crown and church within eight years. The new governor accomplished this task after gathering together many of the people he had brought with him from Spain and Portugal, including Paredes's relatives. But instead of going first to Mexico City and then inland, Carvajal's group went directly to Tampico. Pushing northward late in 1581 into the territories now known as Tamaulipas and Nuevo León, Carvajal founded the present city of Cerralvo (Ciudad de León) and later moved to Saltillo, where he replaced the incumbent officers with some of his own appointees. The reorganization of Saltillo proved to be his downfall. Although the territory was clearly within Carvajal's jurisdiction, the area still belonged to the province of Nueva Viscaya (New Biscay) and was under the captaincy of Alberto de Canto. The authorities of Nueva Viscaya complained to the viceroy of New Spain, Lorenzo Suárez de Mendoza (1518–83), about the jurisdictional dispute. An investigation was soon set in motion, which Carvajal would win before the royal court in 1582.[6] These matters, though, did not sit well with the next viceroy, Alvaro Manríque de Zúniga. Perhaps envious of Carvajal's remarkable success in settling this immense area, the Spanish viceroy was determined to remove the Portuguese governor from his position. Alvaro Manríque y Zúniga hired a Franciscan friar who knew some of Carvajal's relatives in New Spain. The friar was given the task of closely observing the religious activities of this particular group.[7]

Shortly afterward the governor was arrested by the viceroy's soldiers, supposedly over lines of jurisdiction, but the real issue proved to be the governor's Jewish ancestry.[8] After being incarcerated in the royal prison, Carvajal was turned over to the inquisitors on April 14, 1589, on the basis of his niece's testimony.[9] Doña Isabel Rodríguez de Carvajal confessed that she was a practicing Jew and that she observed the law of Moses along with other family members, including her uncle Luis de Carvajal. After many hearings, the governor was found guilty of being "an aider, abetter, harborer, and concealer of apostates to the Holy Catholic Faith."[10] He was stripped of his position and condemned to exile from the New World for a period of six years. The governor is said to have died of "sadness" in 1591, during his first year in prison.[11] All the historical data with regard to the faith of Luis de Carvajal y de la Cueva indicate that he was a devout Christian, although he must have surmised that many of his relatives and close friends, like Paredes's ancestors, were practicing Jews.

During the next 150 years el Nuevo Reino de León, which had prospered under the governorship of Carvajal, experienced many setbacks and became a problem area for the Spanish Crown. The Indians of the region defended their land relentlessly and refused to surrender to the new foreign officials. Their frequent uprisings led to the division of the territory into various Spanish provinces for better defense and settlement. In addition, the colonists were subjected to floods, plagues, and other misfortunes, which forced many of the Jewish settlers to leave the area. The abandonment of the region, coupled with the lack of protection given by the Spanish authorities, left the remaining families in constant conflict with the Indians. As a result, these communities were always armed, and the indomitable spirit of the Indians did not deter them in their efforts to settle in the northern regions of New Spain. In many ways, it was a reflection of the character possessed by the majority of these families that resided in the northern regions of New Spain. They preferred their own kind of freedom, away from Spanish rule, in an effort to establish their own cultural legacy.

In late December 1748 José de Escandón, along with his caravan of predominantly Spanish settlers and *gente de razón* (leading families who considered themselves to be people who used reason), bade farewell to the inhabitants of Querétaro for the journey northeast toward *el río del norte* (the Rio Grande). The newly appointed lieutenant of the viceroy, conquistador, and governor of el Seno Mexicano (the hollow, or recess, between the Panuco and San Antonio rivers) spent an entire year studying the terrain between Tampico and Matagorda Bay for the purpose of colonization. The settlement of this region for the Spanish Crown was necessary for three essential reasons: (1) to protect the Gulf coast from foreign European activities, particularly the French; (2) to fill the gap between the established centers of Tampico and Monterrey to the south and the Texas colony, Bexar (San Antonio), to the north; and (3) to aid the frontier settlements against Indian resistance from the interior.[12] The area had not been colonized because many Indians tribes had found refuge for so many years in the mountainous district of Sierra Madre Oriental (also referred to as Sierra Gorda). Fighting a style of guerrilla warfare, the *chichimecas* (nomads) attacked and raided the small pueblos in the surrounding areas and returned to find asylum in the high mountains, known to the Indians as las Tamaulipas.[13] These free-spirited people refused to give up their lands, which caused many Spanish families to abandon their villages and seek safety in other settled places.

But José de Escandón had his own plans for colonizing the region. Having had some success with his civil method of pacification, as opposed to military force, he proposed a different way of colonization.[14] Escandón abandoned the idea of a Spanish presidio, a military fort established in the frontier regions of New

Spain to protect the settlers against Indian attacks. The region had been sparsely populated in the 1580s by many of Luis de Carvajal's colonists, but the governor of the province of Nuevo Santander still wanted a thorough inspection of the area before any discussion of permanent settlement could take place. His strategy involved the penetration of el Seno Mexicano from various points that form a semicircle extending from Tampico to Bahía. His plan required the aid of other Spanish officials who surrounded el Seno Mexicano, and each captain was required to assemble a division of the most experienced soldiers. These divisions included the units from Tampico, Villa de Valles, Querétaro, Linares, Cerralvo, Coahuila, and Bahía. With the exception of a few units, each division traveled about 150 miles, acquiring data and arriving at the mouth of el río del norte on a specified date.[15] Furthermore, José de Escandón made it clear at the onset that the protection of the Indians was of the utmost importance. Any soldier caught removing an Indian from his lands would suffer grave penalties.[16] The plan of advancing from several directions proved to be quite successful, for each division traveled only a short distance and their small bands allowed them greater mobility. The plan devised by José de Escandón in addition to his excellent leadership validated the council's selection of him for the task of colonizing a vast area of land that had resisted settlement for almost 150 years.

In his colonization project, half of it financed by Escandón himself, the new governor was able to settle the area heretofore known as Nuevo Santander. He proposed to gain the confidence and respect of the Indians instead of using force. His method of *reducción* (reduction) consisted of populating the area with settled families until the nomadic Indians chose to settle, voluntarily. Escandón transported many of the original settlers from the surrounding region and from Querétaro to become the nuclei of the newer ones along el río del norte. These settlers included the families of Américo Paredes and another well-known Chicano writer Rolando Hinojosa. The incentives for relocation included land, money for each family during the first year, and most importantly, independence from the officials of the older establishments.[17] The new official order of these villages was to be imposed by a captain who had military and judicial authority over these settlements. Interestingly, José de Escandón patterned the social structure of these new villages on the existing Indian *rancherías* (ranches)—that is, when a tribe was divided into several units the Indians selected a new chief for that division.[18] Apparently the governor of Nuevo Santander respected the Indians' way of life and gave them the opportunity to be "absorbed into the blood and the culture of the Spanish settlers."[19]

As Américo Paredes showed many years later in his book "*With His Pistol in His Hand,*" Escandón was quite successful in his colonization efforts. The Spaniard established some twenty-two settlements in the province of Nuevo Santander by the end of 1755. More than twelve hundred families settled in this region along *el río bravo* (the Rio Grande), and the first pueblos included Camargo, Reynosa, Mier, Guerrero, and Laredo, a north-bank settlement. The culture in this area was primarily based on the success of a ranching economy where the small landowner lived and worked on his land. Within this patriarchal society, the father or eldest son remained the final authority, although the mother was also well respected. But "obedience depended more on custom and training rather than on force."[20] The people's social conduct, religion, and way of life was transmitted orally from person to person or learned by watching and imitating others. While literacy was valued among the Rio Grande families, the simple pastoral life fostered an oral, traditional culture, and a natural equality among the men.[21]

The people enjoyed telling jokes, listening to stories, and

singing—often to the accompaniment of a guitar—as forms of entertainment. Sometimes they sang *romances*, *décimas*, and *coplas* (types of poetry) brought from old Spain, while at other times they made up their own folk songs. Folk poets composed and performed songs or told stories and jokes about almost any subject imaginable, ranging from horse races and the pitfalls of love, to memorializing the dead. This was a way of sharing and passing on a collective memory of a people, and the importance of the extended family unit kept alive the transmission of these oral traditions. Everyone, especially the elderly, played an active role in the preservation and dissemination of Mexican culture to younger generations.

The ranching way of life proved to be quite advantageous to both Spanish and Indian residents, allowing each of them their own kind of freedom and a measure of self-government. In the coming years, a mestizo culture, or blending of different cultural groups, began to evolve and thrive along the Lower Rio Grande region, away from the Mexican and U.S. governments. Américo Paredes remembered hearing all these things when he was a young boy, and many of these stories were imprinted on him at a very early age. His scholarly research repeated what he already knew about his past history. Paredes did not forget how the "old province of Nuevo Santander was about to emerge from almost a century of isolation and growth, when . . . [a] restless and acquisitive people, exercising the rights of conquest, disturbed the old ways."[22]

U.S. Expansionism

Cultural conflict characterized the impact of North American expansionism on the folklore of the Lower Rio Grande region. The westward movement by the United States began with the purchase of the Louisiana Territory from France in 1803, a land acquisition quickly followed by the official expeditions of Meriwether Lewis and William Clark to the Pacific Northwest (1804) and Zebulon M. Pike to the Great Plains (1806). Lieutenant Pike offered the first major account of contemporary Mexican life in his memoir *An Account of Expeditions* (1810). The lieutenant observed the "hospitality, generosity, and sobriety" of the people, as well as their lack of "national energy, patriotism, enterprise of character, or independence of soul."[23] Pike's latter observation echoes the expansion interests of the United States. Texas was a good place to farm, and the lieutenant's information sparked the interest of many North Americans as they came in search of more land.

The first Anglo-Americans citizens of the province of Texas were the "Texians," a special group of people. They arrived in the region in the early 1820s, led by Moses Austin. The fifty-nine-year-old Missourian was given a contract by Gov. Antonio Martínez of Texas to settle the northern part of the region and create a buffer between the settlers and Indians.[24] When Moses Austin died, his son Stephen continued his father's colonization efforts. With his first contract, Austin relocated about three hundred families ("the old three hundred") at San Felipe de Austin. Between 1824 and 1827 he received five more contracts to bring families to the northern part of Texas. As with José de Escandón's project, families were offered incentives to relocate. In this case, free land on which to raise crops with a minimum of taxation. But quite unlike Escandón, Anglo-Americans were hostile toward the Indians. As T. R. Ferehnbach states, many of these North Americans possessed the old frontier mentality that "the only good Indian [was] a dead Indian."[25] Many of them, moreover, owned African slaves and wanted to transform the new area into another southern slave state.

As wave upon wave of North Americans immigrated into Texas, the young Mexican Republic began to reconsider her initial offer of land. To rectify the situation Mexico officially abolished slavery in 1829 and prohibited any further immigration in 1830. But by that time it was too late. The colonies of Texas expanded rapidly, and Stephen Austin organized "ranging companies" of men to protect the new settlers from Indian attacks. Mexico, moreover, lacked the necessary resources to enforce her laws and slow down this massive immigration.

The original conditions set by the Mexican government, which stated that all immigrants take an oath of allegiance to Mexico and become Catholics, were not followed by the new colonists.[26] The North Americans could not see themselves as subjects of a people they viewed as inferior.[27] In addition, miscegenation within the Mexican culture was not viewed favorably by the Texans.[28] Their early contact with the mestizo folk generated negative stereotypes, and these impressions quickly found their way into written texts. As Stephen Austin's cousin Mary Austin Holley states in her book *Texas: Observations, Historical, Geographical, and Descriptive* (1833), the Mexico-Tejanos "are very ignorant and degraded, and generally speaking, timid and irresolute; and a more brutal and, at the same time, more cowardly set of men does not exist than the Mexican soldiery. They are held in great contempt by the American settlers, who assert that five Indians will chase twenty Mexicans, but five Anglo-Americans will chase twenty Indians. . . . The Mexicans are commonly very indolent, of loose morals, and, if not infidels of which there are many, involved in the grossest superstition."[29] According to Mary Austin Holley, human characteristics were racially determined. She insisted, for example, that Anglo-Americans, Indians, and Mexicans were brave in descending order. The type of writing exemplified in her book "attracted a wide readership—some even achieving best seller status—and laid the foundation for enduring American concepts of Mexican character."[30]

To further complicate matters, local law enforcement and the administration of justice became a serious problem since all the paperwork was sent to the capital of Saltillo, some five hundred miles away from San Felipe de Austin. In spite of these problems, many North Americans complied with the laws of Mexico for the sake of land at a minimum of taxation. These new immigrants had sworn allegiance to Mexico and were Mexican citizens in a practical sense. But the next wave of North Americans would bring the two groups to war.

Mexico's dictator, Antonio López de Santa Anna, caused more harm than good in Texas. Many Texans at first viewed Santa Anna as a friend since he fought against Mexico's centralist form of government. The new settlers thought Texas could gain her own political and economic autonomy as a federalist state. But they changed their minds when Santa Anna reverted to a centralist form of government to preserve Mexico's union. His punitive expedition into Texas and orders to execute the armed rebels at the Alamo and later Goliad were based on his belief that "all the existing laws, whose strict observance the government had just recommended, marked [the rebels] as pirates and outlaws."[31]

These events further alienated the two groups, and when Santa Anna and his troops lost the battle at San Jacinto, the victorious Texans did not forget what had happened at the Alamo, Goliad, and later Mier. In 1836 the newly formed Texas legislature separated itself from Mexico and extended the southern boundary to the mouth of the Rio Grande, even though the original border was the Nueces River.[32] The Mexican parliament was outraged since congress had not recognized the agreements Santa Anna had been forced to sign under duress, and the extension of the southern boundary was understood by most Mexicans as a further affront to their national sovereignty. Although the territory remained "in dispute" for more than a decade, Texans took measures to protect what they believed to be rightfully theirs.

The Texas Rangers officially organized in 1835 to serve as both lawmen and soldiers. Their purpose was to pursue cattle robbers, Indians, and Mexican bandits. Each man was armed with a rifle, knife, and the newly modified Walker Colt, a revolving six-shooter.[33] The pistol gave the Texas Ranger an overwhelming military advantage over the Mexican ranchero who did not even possess firearms. Santa Anna had disarmed the militia after 1835, leaving the frontier settlements at the mercy of the Indians and Texans. The Texas Rangers were crucial in the foundation of the Texas Republic, and they continued to play a prominent role in the war against Mexico as members of the U.S. militia. Along the Lower Rio Grande region, their abuse was never forgotten by the people, and these accounts of the Texas Rangers passed into the Mexican oral history in song and legend.

Pres. James K. Polk's expansionist aims helped set the tone for war with Mexico. He sent Gen. Zachary Taylor and his army "to defend" the Rio Grande in March 1846. Two months later on May 7 and 9, the battles of Palo Alto and Resaca de la Palma were fought, respectively, a few miles from Brownsville, Texas. The U.S.-Mexican War (1846–48) was waged under the doctrine of Manifest Destiny, the God-given right of the United States to take and rule the land occupied by Indians and Mexicans.[34] This attitude resulted in countless cultural conflicts between the North Americans and Mexico-Tejano population. The war cry "Remember the Alamo! Remember Goliad!" rationalized future U.S. land seizures in the Nueces–Rio Grande region and other parts of Greater Mexico. The Mexican people were humiliated when their territory was taken, and then they were subjected to abuse. Even Gen. Winfield Scott conceded that his countrymen "committed atrocities to make Heaven weep and every American of Christian morals blush for his country. . . . Murder, robbery and rape of mothers and daughters in the presence of tied-up males of the families have been common all along the Rio Grande."[35] The worst victims of the U.S.-Mexican War were the Mexican citizens themselves. Their political ties with Mexico were effectively broken, and they endured abuses by the victorious Americans. When the Treaty of Guadalupe Hidalgo was signed on February 2, 1848, a border now separated the blood-related families that had lived for nearly a hundred years along both banks of the Lower Rio Grande. Fear and mistrust of North Americans endured for many years, for these people who were now considered to be neither from Mexico nor from the United States.

The border folk did not wait long to express their resentment. Juan Nepomuceno "Cheno" Cortina, a member of the land-owning elite, was one of the first Mexican "bandits" to rebel against North American rule. In 1859 a drunken ranchero was being beaten with the butt of a pistol by Robert Shears, a Brownsville city marshal. Cheno defended the Mexican cowhand whom he knew from his mother's ranch. An altercation ensued and Cortina shot and wounded the city marshal.[36] Seeking protection from Anglo authorities, Cheno crossed the border to Matamoros, Tamaulipas. Many Mexicans viewed Cortina as a champion of his people and banded together with Cheno to raid Texas border towns. Juan Nepomuceno Cortina became a general in the Mexican army, governor of the state of Tamaulipas, and later a prisoner of Pres. Porfirio Díaz in Mexico City. After he was released, Cheno Cortina returned to his old ways—creating havoc for Texas authorities and continuing his own method of cattle retrieval—until the end of his life in 1892.

From a Mexican Ranching Way of Life to a U.S. Capitalist Economy

Many export-oriented North Americans understood the commercial importance of the Lower Rio Grande valley and the port trade it offered in the town of Matamoros. As Anglo merchants and lawyers moved into the area, the way of life of the rancho began to change. An air of distrust persisted—notwithstanding intermarriage and its institution of *compadrazgo*, a religious custom where two families became related to one another as adopted godparents of a baptized child.[37] Thus, the new North American elite became "Mexicanized" when they assimilated some of the cultural values and traditions of the border folk. The Anglo ranchers began to learn the tricks of the trade of the Mexican landowner and his paternal bond with the *vaquero* (ranch hand or cowboy) and *peón* (laborer without a horse, or on foot). In doing so, the new ranchers counted on the protection of their hired hands from the so-called treacherous Mexicans; while the hired Mexican working class, in turn, would count on their new bosses for protection from Anglo authorities, vigilantes, and outlaws. This "peace structure" allowed the new northern arrivals to accommodate themselves to an established sociopolitical order while simultaneously displacing the Mexican landowners. As the folklorist Jovita González stated in her master's thesis, "Social Life in Cameron, Starr, and Zapata Counties" (1930), intermarriage provided a convenient way to contain Anglo military victory when Mexican daughters were "married at an early age, and not for love, but for family connections."[38] The union between North American men and Mexican women was a pattern that would be followed throughout the U.S. Southwest.

In time, the old feudal system with its roots in the Spanish heritage of Mexico was replaced with a capitalist society. If the old

Mexican families of the region saw their land as their traditional patrimony, the Anglo elite viewed it as the basis for business enterprise. The ranching way of life that had absorbed the *fuereño* (outsiders) from the south and the *gringo* from the north for approximately 150 years could no longer exist because of pressures from northern foreign influences. This economic and cultural shift took place from about 1900 to 1920. Three principal factors can be attributed to the transformation of the Lower Rio Grande region from a simple ranching economy into a multimillion dollar industry: (1) the arrival of the railroad; (2) the growth of the irrigation business; and (3) the influx of refugees from the Mexican revolution (1910–20). While the power and prestige of the old aristocratic families diminished, the new Anglo ruling class and Mexican laborers became more polarized.

The development of the railroad in 1904 made travel more convenient and facilitated the transport of products to and from the once-isolated communities along the Lower Rio Grande. The railroad brought many new arrivals from the Midwest who were lured into the area by promises of quick money. The midwesterners, though, did not intermingle with the Mexican population and made little effort to understand their way of life. According to Emilio C. Forto, a resident of Brownsville for fifty years and former sheriff, county judge, and secretary of the School Board of Trustees for the City of Brownsville, "ninety per cent of the Americans [did] not appear to understand and [did] not seem to care to learn the customs or respect the ideals of the Mexicans."[39] Eventually, many new arrivals positioned themselves in local governments and began to voice their desire for paved roads, market facilities, and their own private schools.

The northerners also brought with them manufactured products like the steam pump and lifts to facilitate agriculture and irrigation. The industrial development of farms and the new political institutions governed by North Americans displaced many rancheros and the old Mexican elite from their lands. New taxes, cash offers, diversion of water, coercion, and fraud soon reduced the number of Mexican landowners.[40] The old patriarchal and paternal relationship between *el patrón* (owner) and peón dwindled, as did the practice of intermarriage among Anglos and Mexico-Tejanos. The new entrepreneurs transformed the economy and culture of the Lower Rio Grande region.

Mexico's revolution only worsened the border folks' problems as waves of poor refugees moved northward into south Texas. The flow of immigrants created a surplus of cheap labor for the North American farmer and a natural division between him and the Mexican laborer. But this was only part of the problem for Mexico-Tejanos. Because of Mexico's civil strife, a window of opportunity was created for the south Texas landowner in terms of water flow. Farmers were able to successfully lobby the U.S. government for many irrigation projects that diverted most of the dependable stream of water away from Mexican territories and into the United States.[41] Thus, in a matter of years, the Rio Grande valley became a paradise of fertile acres of cotton, sugarcane, cereal corn, and citrus trees, while in the state of Tamaulipas the dry land was barely able to cultivate beans, rice, cotton, and sugarcane.[42] Food grows where water flows, and capital follows crops. This boom in commercial agriculture marked the beginning of U.S. big business in the Lower Rio Grande valley and an end to its traditional ranching economy.

Texas' new elite created an economic system that was designed to protect their interests as farmers and to exclude the border folk. As more and more rancheros began to lose their land, and vaqueros, tenants, and artisans were displaced from their jobs, many Mexico-Tejanos felt that they had no other choice but to fight, thus transforming the Lower Rio Grande valley into a virtual war zone between 1915 and 1917. The armed insurrection by the border folk was their way of saying *¡Basta ya!* (Enough is enough!) to the so-called fortune makers in south Texas.

The border folk's insurrection was branded by North American newspapers and politicians as "Mexican banditry." But for the rebels it was an attempt to regain control of their lands in south Texas. Their manifesto, "El Plan de San Diego," called for (1) an uprising on February 20, 1915, by the Liberating Army of Races and People (composed of Mexicans, Negroes, Japanese, and Indians), (2) an end to "Yankee tyranny," and (3) the creation of an independent republic that would consist of Texas, New Mexico, Arizona, Colorado, and California. According to James A. Sandos's *Rebellion in the Borderlands* (1992), the anger of the border folk was so extreme that a "race war [was] envisioned—with every North American male over the age of sixteen to be put to death."[43] As houses and farms were destroyed and a train was derailed outside of Brownsville, Texas, local Anglo residents began to take action. Once again they called on the Texas Rangers to suppress the raids in south Texas. These lawmen, instead of attempting to restore order, threatened the border folk. "If you are found here in the next five days you will be dead!"[44] And indeed the Texas Rangers killed many innocent Mexicans on the pretext that they were suspects "attempting to escape."[45]

The abuses of the ranger force left a lasting legacy of mistrust with the border folk. The late Texan historian Walter Prescott Webb, in his well-known book *The Texas Rangers: A Century of Frontier Defense* (1935), declares that the "orgy of bloodshed" caused by the Texas Rangers, local posses, and peace officers "has been estimated at five hundred and at five thousand, but the actual number can never be known."[46] Benjamin Heber Johnson, another Texan historian, states that the "discovery of skeletons even decades later suggest[s] that a number in the low thousands is probable."[47] Lynching and executions became so common that the *San Antonio Express* stopped reporting the loss of Mexican lives.[48] Frank Pierce, another historian, asserted that "during the bandit raids of 1915 many evil influences were brought to bear to clear the country of the Mexicans."[49] The wealth created for a small group of people came at the expense of many innocent lives. Moreover, "the defeat of the Plan de San Diego," as Benjamin H. Johnson points out, "ushered in a system of harsh racial segregation in south Texas, one explicitly modeled on the south's Jim Crow."[50] The victory allowed North Americans in Texas to further disenfranchise the border folk, limiting their rights as U.S. citizens and establishing segregation in public schools and other places. It was while these battles were being waged along the Lower Rio Grande region that Américo Paredes was born in Brownsville, Texas.

Early Images of Mexicans in Literature and Folklore Studies

Although the U.S.-Mexican War officially ended in 1848, the cultural and psychological effects of the conflict continued for years to come. The secession of Texas produced an impressive corpus of North American literature characterized by anti-Mexican rhetoric. Prejudice against the Mexican people informs volumes of letters, memoirs, dime novels, and Texas romances. Mexicans are portrayed as degenerates who oscillate between docility and treachery.[51] The satisfaction expressed in southwestern novels and travel books about the expansion of the United States in Mexican territory is profound, and the stereotypes of Mexican people in such works had a lasting effect.

Américo Paredes demonstrated in his book *"With His Pistol in His Hand"* that prejudicial views against Mexicans had not diminished almost one hundred years later. He quoted what Walter

Prescott Webb (1888–1963) thought about the Mexican in the mid-1930s: "Without disparagement, it may be said that there is a cruel streak in the Mexican nature, or so the history of Texas would lead one to believe. This cruelty may be a heritage from the Spanish of the Inquisition; it may, and doubtless should be, attributed partly to the Indian blood. . . . The Mexican warrior . . . was, on the whole, inferior to the Comanche and wholly unequal to the Texan. The whine of the leaden slugs stirred in him an irresistible impulse to travel with rather than against the music. He won more victories over the Texans by parley than by force of arms. For making promises—and for breaking them—he had no peer."[52] These attitudes were expressed throughout the American Southwest. If prejudice had been prevalent before the war, in time of warfare the rhetoric intensified. It informed war propaganda, and it was disseminated after the war in historical, sociological, and literary works.[53] The successful dissemination of stereotypical views about the Mexican had an impact on the lives and psyches of Mexican Americans. As many Mexicans were assimilating to the political hegemony of the United States, their identity was affected to some extent by what Anglo-Americans thought and understood about them.

Américo Paredes directed much of his scholarly efforts at countering the negative attitudes and prejudicial views toward the Mexican American people and offering what he considered to be a more objective assessment of the matter. But scarce literature from a Mexican American experience made it difficult to counter these conservative attitudes. Thus, he celebrated his people's oral traditions to reconstruct the history and delineate the picture of Mexican Americans. The field of folklore became a platform for Américo Paredes in his attempts to dignify the common and spiritual life of the Mexican American people. Although even this discipline was not free from pejorative Mexican interpretations.

The American Folklore Society was established in 1888 and published its own periodical, the *Journal of American Folklore*. The folklorist's role was to seek out, observe, collect, and describe the traditional practices (physical and verbal) of a particular group or community. As a historical science, one of its main objectives was to reproduce a people's past—a past that was inevitably tied to tradition: "information and belief handed down from generation to generation without the use of writing."[54] In Texas a regional folk society was established in 1909 to collect its own brand of folklore. Though never a despotic organization, the Texas Folklore Society was primarily an Anglo-dominated operation that leaned toward a literary orientation and popular audiences, and disliked any allegiance to "scientific" folklore.[55] For celebrated folklorists like John A. Lomax (1867–1948) and J. Frank Dobie (1888–1964), the region served as a basis for "Texian" local identity, and ethnic minorities functioned as its local color. The result was a condescending view of these cultural groups as "folk," a people who possessed no desire to better themselves or their lot.[56] In fact, one of the basic features of colonial discourse in the representation of otherness is its dependence on a "fixed" type.[57] Rather than promote change or adaptation of a people, this manner of description seeks out uniformity and simplicity as a method of dominance and control. The lack of perspective displayed by folklorists like J. Frank Dobie and his followers with regard to the Mexican character served to perpetuate Mexican stereotypes.[58] Mexican informants were described as docile, untrustworthy, and superstitious. Moreover, the lack of familiarity with the linguistic and cultural subtleties of the ordinary people who served as Mexican informants flawed regionalist interpretation.

A case in point is the folk song "Versos de los Bandidos," cited by J. Frank Dobie in his article "*Versos* of the Texas *Vaqueros*." Dobie refers to a variant of the "Corrido de los Sediciosos" (Ballad of the Seditionists), which relates the 1915 Mexico-Tejano insurrection led by Aniceto Pizaña.[59] But as Américo Paredes would later demonstrate, the variant collected by Dobie ridicules the seditionists and glorifies the Texas Rangers.[60] The Anglo-American's misreading of the text was due in part to his ignorance of performance within the ethnographic exchange. It is difficult to determine what purpose the performer or performers had in mind with this ballad without properly understanding the total performance situation. It may have been that these Mexican singers were hiding behind the mask of public compliance and faking it, so to speak. This suggests that J. Frank Dobie's fieldwork method was poor and that his interpretation of Mexican American folklore, collected via fieldwork, was inaccurate. In other words, the ethnographic component of folklore research at this time lacked descriptive detail in its re-creation of a Mexican American oral tradition.

Another interesting example is the Mexican folktale "La Cucaracha," a story included in the book *Puro Mexicano* (1935) edited by J. Frank Dobie. According to Riley Aiken, the collector of the tale, the Mexican informant Doroteo lived on a ranch thirty miles north of Brownsville, Texas. This is the only piece of information we have about this person living along the Lower Rio Grande border.[61]

"La Cucaracha" narrates the tale of Juan de Toluca, "a good man" who dies and cannot enter the kingdom of heaven because he is a Mexican. Saint Peter explains to him that nowhere was it written that heaven was made for Mexicans. Juan, therefore, plays a trick. He claims to have lost his sombrero and will never leave until he finds it. Saint Peter opens the gates of Paradise and Juan de Toluca loses himself in the crowd of people. Afterward, three angels complain to the Lord that they have lost a ring, a diamond brooch, and earbobs, respectively. Each suspects that a certain individual has these items and the Lord says, "I believe there is a Mexican in heaven." God then asks Saint Peter to find a Texan since "he knows the Mexican." The Texan relates to the Lord the weaknesses of the Mexican—women, tequila, the song "La Cucaracha," and his native land. God promptly has a French violinist play the song "La Cucaracha":

> La cucaracha, la cucaracha,
> Ya no puede navegar.
> Porque le faltan, porque le faltan
> Sus patitas de detrás.
>
> The cockroach, the cockroach,
> can no longer navigate.
> Because he is missing, because he is missing
> his little hind feet. (Author's translation)

Someone suddenly yells from the crowd, "*¡Viva México!*" The Lord then has Saint Peter remove Juan de Toluca from heaven. The tale ends as follows: "And that is the true story, *amigo*, of the only Mexican who ever went to heaven, and you see why they kicked him out."[62]

Doroteo's rendition of the tale is important for folklorists and cultural anthropologists, alike. On one level it appears to be a story about a "dumb" Mexican; yet on another, "La Cucaracha" can be an ironic representation of the Mexican stereotype and a recognition of this stereotype by the Mexico-Tejano informant—an important point overlooked by Riley Aiken and J. Frank Dobie in *Puro Mexicano*. Apparently neither was aware of Doroteo as a potential performer of folklore because the context of the story was not taken into account. This idea of folklore as performance in relation to Mexican stereotypes suggests the pervasiveness of negative stereotypes and a recognition and adaptation of these labels by the informant. It is difficult to completely appreciate the border Mexican's rendition of the tale, since there is nothing written about his oral performance. In order to make this folk item partially intelligible for others, more information is needed to place it in its proper cultural context. For instance, how was the story related to the interaction that preceded and followed it? To what extent did the audience participate in the performance? What were some of the effects of the border Mexican's performance on the audience? When and where did the performance take place? And what group or groups were involved at the time the story was told? That the border Mexican was poking fun at the outsider might have been clear if more had been said about the context of the performance.

Three of the most important Mexican American predecessors for Américo Paredes in folklore were Aurelio M. Espinosa and Arthur L. Campa in New Mexico and Jovita González in Texas. Each sought to offer an impartial account of views regarding Mexican Americans to counter those that they knew were inaccurate and prejudicial.

The founder of modern Mexican American folklore scholarship is Aurelio Macedonio Espinosa (1880–1958), a scholar trained at the University of Chicago. For almost the entire first half of the twentieth century, he demonstrated his enthusiasm for the study of New Mexican folklore, including the Spanish language. Espinosa's academic training was rigorous (by the academic standards of his time), and he traveled extensively throughout the Southwest (and later Spain) in search of his material. He dedicated himself to being well prepared for the discipline. Some of the prerequisites Espinosa demanded of himself included a thorough knowledge of the Spanish dialect spoken in the region, of Spanish literature and history, and of modern and classical languages for a comparative study of the material collected, and an awareness of the social sciences, since history, anthropology, and social psychology all relate in one way or another to the field of folklore.[63]

Espinosa's pioneering works in folklore, such as "New-Mexican Spanish Folk-Lore" published in the *Journal of American Folklore* (1910–16) and *Cuentos populares españoles* (1923–26), underscored the Spanish peninsular elements of the New Mexican culture. Many of these collections dealt with folk narratives, although one in particular did concern itself with the anecdote, a type of narrative not commonly published by folklorists of the time. In his efforts to collect folklore material from Spanish-speaking Americans, the New Mexican scholar wanted to reflect a "civilization that [was] basically and fundamentally Spanish."[64] Aurelio Espinosa thought he could give a certain air of dignity to the folklore of the people of Mexican origin by highlighting their European heritage. He compared the folklore of Spain with that of the American Southwest to find similarities, specifically in northern New Mexico and southern Colorado. In his efforts to counteract the North Americans' contention that the Mexicans were inferior, Espinosa wanted to show that they were fundamentally Spanish. His comparative approach emphasized the origin and spread of folklore items (such as tales and ballads), and made use of the "historic-geographic," or "Finnish," method with stress on the way that folk material travels from region to region. He said little about the life of the people.

In his study and collection of folklore data, Espinosa discovered that a vast treasure was to be found in Texas, New Mexico, California, and Arizona, not to mention all of Mexico and Spanish America.[65] He was convinced that most of the folklore material found in the oral tradition of New Mexico and southern Colorado had its origins in Spain, having undergone little change since the arrival of the early sixteenth- and seventeenth-century Spanish settlers. As early as 1911 Espinosa was certain "that practically all the New-Mexican Spanish folk-lore material is traditional; i.e., its sources are to be found in the Spain of the fifteenth to the seventeenth century. . . . This, I believe, is true of the folk-tales, as it is true of the ballads, proverbs, riddles, nursery rhymes, *coplas*, myths, superstitions, and other folk-lore material. . . . The fact that the folklore material from New Mexico is practically all traditional makes its study of great importance, as it helps to interpret better general Spanish folk-lore, and is also a key to the interpretation of the problem of the progress and change of the old material as it has been preserved in the oral tradition of the New Mexicans for some three hundred years."[66] Aurelio Espinosa thought he offered convincing evidence in favor of his views by publishing collections of traditional folk literature in the region and later by comparing them with published materials on the folk literature of Spain, Spanish America, and other European countries. One of his most significant folktale studies was on the "tar baby" story. Espinosa's analysis of 152 versions of this story from all over the world and his conclusion that its origin can be traced to India exemplified his comparative approach to folklore. He was mostly concerned with the origins and diffusion of songs and tales, or with their "biographies," so to speak. Aurelio Espinosa's major contributions to the field of Spanish dialectology and folk literature included the publication of more than one hundred books, monographs, and articles.[67] His emphasis on the essentially Spanish character of this material had a tremendous impact on the development of Mexican American folklore.

Aurelio Espinosa's good intentions, however, did not succeed in offering a view that captured the human experience of the Mexican American people because his collection of folklore items was narrow. He ignored aspects of style and artistry, creation and alterations, influences of other cultures, social context, and individual genius within the repertoire of the folklore of northern New Mexico and southern Colorado. And as Américo Paredes would later point out, the New Mexican scholar was seldom concerned with the presence of Mexican folklore.[68]

From around 1930 to 1975, Arthur León Campa (1905–78) continued the efforts initiated by Aurelio Espinosa to understand the folklore of the Hispanic Southwest. The Columbia-trained scholar's most important achievement, *Hispanic Culture in the Southwest*, was published posthumously in 1979. Unlike Espinosa's more literary approach to the folklore of this area, Campa focused his attention on the common people. He thought there was a popular culture that was significant and germane to the region, and he disagreed with Aurelio Espinosa's premise that the Mexican people of the American Southwest were fundamentally and culturally Spanish. Campa characterized such views as a "Spanish fantasy" and felt that it was "nonsense before the facts which history presents":[69] "The Spanish speaking people of the Southwest are not so conscious of Spain as one would be led to believe by overly enthusiastic folklorists. Few of them came directly from Spain. The soldiery originated in Mexico . . . ; furthermore, it is not in keeping with Spanish character to be strongly attached to a country in which they no longer live. . . . In the nineteen years that I have spent in the Southwest, nowhere have I heard any allusions to 'El Cid,' and I believe it is stretching the imagination too far to try to make Spain out of a country that was called *Nuevo México*."[70] Campa argued that New Mexican folklore was fundamentally Mexican. He was not interested in finding linguistic and folklore commonalties between Spain and the Hispanic Southwest; he was interested in finding commonalties with Mexico. Campa did not view the cultural regions of northern New Mexico and southern Colorado as especially different from other Hispanic settlements in the United States; rather he sought to link all the

Spanish-speaking colonies throughout the Southwest and Mexico.[71] For Arthur Campa, understanding the folklore of New Mexico, Colorado, Arizona, California, and Texas was a way to contribute to a synthesis of a Mexican culture conceived in broad terms.

His rejection of one cultural label for another forced him to address the issue of Mexican American identity. He attempted to address the question of identity and self-determination by emphasizing the political, cultural, and linguistic complexities of the Mexican American people of the Southwest:

> Obviously they are not Mexicans, and they have not been since 1848; neither are they natives exclusively. Few can prove conclusively to be of Spanish descent, and none of them are Spanish Americans, considering that such an adjective applies to people in Spanish America. On the other hand, there are valid reasons why New Mexicans may claim in part any or all the foregoing appellations. Legally and nationally they are Americans; linguistically, Spanish; Spanish American, geographically; culturally, Mexican; native by birth, and New Mexican by state boundaries. What are they racially, since that seems to be of so great concern? The answer to that question may be found in the history of the conquest.[72]

Campa believed that neither the Spanish linguistic nor cultural heritage nor the political status of the southwest people as Americans was the determining factor for identity. For him it was the Mexican culture that accounted for the identity of the people of the Hispanic Southwest. His efforts were directed at emphasizing the Mexican element of this culture. Campa, moreover, wanted the people of the region to educate themselves in order to empower their communities as Mexican communities.[73] Part of this education involved what he referred to as the "urbanization" of a rural people, so that they could acquire the technical competence and cultural values of a progressive society.[74] Although he did recognize cultural differences, even conflict, between North Americans and Mexicans, Campa concluded that a cultural coexistence could take place if the two were willing to better understand and respect each other. The "new civilization" would serve as the model of cultural pluralism in North America and Latin America.[75]

Arthur Campa's cultural synthesis of the Hispanic Southwest stressed a comprehensive historical view of Spanish exploration and settlement. He emphasized the "mission-pueblo-presidio" model of colonization that laid the foundation for a pastoral culture throughout New Spain's far northern frontier. Campa's broad approach to this vast territory caused him, however, to minimize specific historical events like the U.S.-Mexican War and to oversimplify specific folklore items such as the corrido.

In the 1920s and 1930s, around the same time that Arthur Campa initiated his work in Mexican American cultural studies, Jovita González (1899–1983) in Texas began to publish her folklore articles. As a native of the Lower Rio Grande region and a member of the Mexican upper middle class, González studied and worked with J. Frank Dobie at the University of Texas at Austin.[76] In 1930 she completed her master's thesis titled "Social Life in Cameron, Starr, and Zapata Counties" at the University of Texas at Austin where she discussed the people's lives, the history of the region, and the cultural transformation that took place as a result of North American expansionism. Her assessment of the Mexico-Tejano culture is impressive, and there are several instances when she alluded to conflict between the Mexican and North American cultures. Jovita González ends her study by claiming that the educated children of Texas Mexicans will be "the converging element of two antagonistic civilizations . . . [that] will bring to an end the racial feuds that have existed in the border for nearly a century."[77]

In "Tales and Songs of Mexicans" (1930) González again suggests a conflict between the two cultures by observing the presence of *tragedias* (sad folk songs) among the Mexican vaqueros. She was not convinced that the protagonists of these ballads were all bandits.[78] They were heroes for the Mexican people, and one of the best-known tragedias was about Juan Nepomuceno Cortina.[79] In another article, "America Invades the Border Towns" (1930), González discusses the cultural forces in the Lower Rio Grande region and even claims that the *peones* (laborers on foot) benefited from the North American capitalist system.[80] And as she does in her master's thesis, she concludes her essay with the hope that the younger generations of Mexico-Tejanos "will bring to an end the racial feuds that have existed along the border for nearly a century."[81] Her scholarship influenced Américo Paredes because, in his own words, she was "one of the first Mexican Americans to write in English about her own people."[82] Yet in her work she fails to note the differences between the corrido and décima forms, and her relationship with J. Frank Dobie and the Texas Folklore Society may have limited her intellectual pursuits.[83]

Aurelio M. Espinosa, Arthur L. Campa, and Jovita González were all forerunners of Américo Paredes, whose contribution was to underscore the specificity of the people of the American Southwest. But they did not fully capture the common and spiritual life of the Mexican people in the United States. If certain elements of the Mexican American repertoire belonged to the shared traditions of Greater Mexico, that was only half the picture for Américo Paredes. The other half was generated in social opposition to a foreign culture. This folklore—unique in its own way from that of Mexico—emerged out of conflict, struggle, and resistance. To neglect such items in Mexican American folklore was, in Paredes's view, a serious error: "A certain mistaken delicacy, or the desire not to offend, not to bring up painful matters which we all know have existed and which we all want to remedy, has convinced some folklorists that it would be in poor taste to expose the conflict between the Mexican and North American cultures. But this is to deny folklore study its place as a scholarly discipline. It belongs with the opinion that anyone who studies obscene folklore is an obscene person and that anyone who studies popular beliefs must be superstitious as well."[84] In efforts to understand the nature and mind-set of Mexican Americans, North American folklorists had failed to consider the clash of cultures as an important factor in the lives of these citizens. Américo Paredes believed that to fully appreciate the character of Mexican Americans, folklorists needed to acknowledge the imposition of another way of life on a people who possessed their own culture, language, and history. To ignore such a fact was a mistake in the collection and interpretation of folklore. Paredes knew that more careful analysis of this conflict, in its natural setting and with the folk poet in mind, was necessary to grasp the spirit of this particular community.

Chapter 2

His Life and Work

Porque a mí me importa un bledo que me apunten
con el dedo,
que de mí murmure quedo tu correcta sociedad;
pueblo bajo y barullero, pueblo dulce y romancero,
yo te juro que te quiero,
yo te quiero de verdad.
—Américo Paredes, "Mi pueblo"

Américo Paredes Manzano, the son of Justo Paredes Cisneros and Clotilde Manzano Vidal, was born on September 3, 1915, in Brownsville, Texas, in the peak months of the racial wars between North Americans and Mexico-Tejanos.[1] The fifth child of a family of eight, six men and two women, he was named after Amerigo Vespucci, the Italian navigator.[2]

How Américo Paredes's Life Was Shaped along the Lower Rio Grande Border

As a boy, he spent most of his summers with his relatives across the Rio Grande in Matamoros, Tamaulipas. There, in a rural Mexican environment, he learned about the music and history of his people. Don Justo, an anticlerical ranchero and former border rebel, imparted to his son many of the beliefs and customs of a ranching way of life in evident decline. On many occasions, Don Justo sat and talked for hours with Américo about the ways of his father, grandfather, and great-grandfather. The oral tradition transmitted from generation to generation in many families like his own was at the heart of a culture Américo Paredes would be instrumental in understanding and explaining to others. Among the ballads, tales, and jests were the legendary accounts of Juan Nepomuceno Cortina along the Rio Grande border; Catarino Garza's clashes with Mexican and U.S. forces; José Mosqueda's train robbery outside Brownsville, Texas; and Gregorio Cortez's self-defense "with his pistol in his hand" against an Anglo sheriff. Folklore as performance fascinated Américo as a boy, and it became an important concept in much of his writing.

Before enrolling in an English-speaking elementary school in Texas, Américo could already read and write in Spanish. His teachers were his father and his eldest brother, Eliseo. The Paredes family recognized early on Américo's inquisitive nature, and they had high expectations for him. "Este es él que va a hacer algo por nosotros, por nuestra familia. Es él que va a ir a la escuela," his father was often heard commenting to his friends.[3] The high expectations weighed on Américo's conscience and played a role in his growing sense of responsibility toward his family and toward the people along the Lower Rio Grande border.

In elementary school Américo took to reading and writing in English with enthusiasm. The quiet life of the rancho away from school offered minimal distractions during these years. He enjoyed reading popular literature for children including the Tarzan books of Edgar Rice Burroughs, but he also read literary works in both Spanish and English. He was especially fond of his book of Shakespeare's sonnets, a gift from his brother Eliseo. Books became his companions. They allowed him to dream of other worlds, and they were an invitation to explore his own fantasy world. Américo remembered spending hours re-creating the stories he heard from the old men or making up his own, imagining he was Gregorio Cortez fighting against the *rinches* (Texas Rangers). Daydreaming allowed him to project himself as a hero of his people and helped him relieve his anger and frustration with the reality of the Mexico-Tejano border folk.

His father's interest in Spanish language poetry also influenced the young Américo's literary formation. Don Justo Paredes memorized, read, and even wrote poetry, and he would often recite his own décima or *espinela*, *redondilla*, or *canto a desafío*.[4] The décima cantada, a popular ballad form in New Spain, was not always accompanied by music. For Américo Paredes it was "the narrative, which the *décimas* adorned like colorful motifs on a larger design—the narrative was the important thing because it bound the *décimas* together, and all of [the people] as well."[5]

The ability to read and write effectively in two languages naturally broadened his horizons at a young age. The informal education received at home combined with the more formal one in the Brownsville public school system gave Américo a dual perspective. He appreciated his formal schooling, but he did not hesitate to challenge the information he received in the classroom if it conflicted with what he learned at home. As his sister and others have recalled, he was generally a quiet and mild-mannered individual.[6] But he was not afraid to stand up for his culture, his background. Américo said he protested to the point of becoming unruly when his teachers offered a view of recent history he considered denigrating to his people. In junior high school, for example, Américo Paredes remembered the time his teacher tried to justify the creation of the Monroe Doctrine. The teacher told a story to the class about a little boy with a lollipop who met a bigger boy:

"Suppose . . . [this] big bully comes over and tries to take it away from the little boy. Then the United States is the other boy that comes and beats up the bully." At that moment Américo asked: "Yes, but what if the boy after he beats up the bully starts beating up the boy with the lollipop and takes it away?"[7] According to Américo Paredes, the class celebrated his point with laughter, and he was sent to the principal's office for insubordination.

While attending junior high school, Américo developed another of his many interests—his love for music. One of his favorite musicians was the singer and guitar player Ignacio "Nacho" Montelongo, a border Mexican who would pile his clothes and belongings into an old washtub, swim the Rio Grande, and sing and play for the Paredes family. Years later Nacho would be recalled by Américo as Chano Quintana, a memorable character in the short story "Rebeca" (1994).

Nacho Montelongo taught the young Américo to play the guitar, although don Justo was adamantly opposed to the idea. Américo's father had a distaste for popular musicians, whom he considered irresponsible and bohemian. His image of the popular musician was Juventino Rosas (1868–94), the composer of a celebrated song entitled "Sobre las olas" (Over the Waves). Don Justo would often remind his son that he had met Mr. Rosas in Monterrey, Nuevo León, and if he saw him once dressed in a fine suit, conducting an orchestra, he also saw Mr. Rosas lying in the streets *borracho* (drunk). Américo's father was convinced that all musicians were drunks and that "they were all a lost cause."[8]

Disagreement between father and son over the issue of popular music is the central theme in one of Paredes's first short stories, quite appropriately titled "Over the Waves Is Out" (1953). He would later learn to play the piano, which was another of his childhood dreams. Many years later Américo was surprised to learn that his father had played the guitar, until his father's father forced him to abandon his own musical pursuits.

Despite don Justo's wishes, Américo secretly purchased a cheap guitar and began to compose songs at the same time that he began to write poetry. He visited musicians and poets along the border to practice, write, and sing. Sometimes these artists would cross the border to Matamoros and meet at a lodge called the Texas Bar. Food and drink were cheap there, and a group of about eight to ten members gathered outside in the patio area to recite their own poetry. Other times Américo and his friends drove around Brownsville and frequented different places to sing and write poetry. Paredes became so adept at composing songs and playing the guitar that he was hired to perform on the radio for fifteen dollars a week.[9]

Américo Paredes pursued his love for reading and writing in high school. Often, his unconventional views were not well received by his teachers. Américo remembered having written an essay in high school on William Shakespeare's *Merchant of Venice* (1603). Paredes read the play in terms of his own situation, and he sympathized with Shylock's precarious reality as a Jew in a Christian world. In a 1984 interview Américo Paredes recalled a famous passage from the play that he believed had significance to the Mexico-Tejanos of the Río Grande border: "If you prick us, do we not bleed? if you tickle us, do we not laugh? if you poison us, do we not die? and if you wrong us, shall we not revenge? if we are like you in the rest, we will resemble you in that. If a Jew wrong a Christian, what is his humility? revenge: if a Christian wrong a Jew, what should his sufferance be by Christian example? why, revenge. The villainy you teach me, I will execute; and it shall go hard but I will better the instruction."[10] One can see how the young Paredes could read into this passage the frustrations and predicaments of Mexicans living in the United States. In the same interview Américo Paredes commented that other teachers and even members of the community had heard about his essay.[11] He was aware that writing could be an effective tool to challenge conventional views, and he was determined to be well read in both Spanish and English literature.

Américo Paredes remembered reading a variety of Spanish poetry in "Lunes Literarios de la Prensa," a literary supplement published by the daily *La Prensa* of San Antonio, Texas. He read well-known poets like Gustavo Adolfo Bécquer, José Santos Chocano, and Rubén Darío among many others. In English he read the poetry of Henry Wadsworth Longfellow, Walt Whitman, and Edgar Allan Poe. He received inspiration from this poetry and tried to apply it to his own social reality along the Lower Rio Grande border. He knew that his poetry would address the border folk's social and economic situation, but he had not yet found what I would characterize as a distinctive Chicano voice of resistance. There is an artificiality to some of his poetry, such as the poem "Flute Song" (1935):

Flute Song

Why was I ever born
Heir to a people's sorrow
Wishing this day were done
And yet fearful for the morrow.

Why was I ever born
Proud of my southern race,
If I must seek my sun
In an Anglo-Saxon face.

Wail, wail, oh flutes, your dismal tune,
The agony of our birth;
Better perhaps had I never known
That you lived upon the earth.[12]

Although a sense of humiliation torments the poet who despises North American exploitation, the poem seems awkward for a young Chicano activist with verses like "fearful of the morrow" and "Wail, wail, oh flutes, your dismal tune." The poetry does not possess any notable qualities that set it apart from other English verses, and it is difficult to imagine Américo Paredes with this type of attitude, given his background and personality. The verses are dull, "weak," and "uninspiring."[13]

A poem that illustrates the dilemma of an in-between existence, the essence of a divided reality, is "The Mexico-Texan" (1935). Paredes recalled writing this particular piece "while walking the 21 blocks home from [high] school" in the spring of 1934.[14] A vernacular and sympathetic voice is used to explain the Mexico-Tejano's predicament:

The Mexico-Texan

The Mexico-Texan he's one fonny man
Who leeves in the region that's north of the Gran',
Of Mexican father he born in these part,
And sometimes he rues it dip down in he's heart.

For the Mexico-Texan he no gotta lan',
He stomped on the neck on both sides of the Gran',
The dam gringo lingo he no cannot spik,
It twisters the tong and it make you fill sick.

A cit'zen of Texas they say that he ees,
But then, why they call him the Mexican Grease?
Soft talk and hard action, he can't understan',
The Mexico-Texan he no gotta lan'.

If he cross the reever, eet ees just as bad,
On high poleeshed Spanish he break up his had,
American customs those people no like,
They hate that Miguel they should call him El Mike,
And Mexican-born, why they jeer and they hoot,
"Go back to the gringo! Go lick at hees boot!"
In Texas he's Johnny, in Mexico Juan,
But the Mexico-Texan he no gotta lan'.

Elactions come round and the gringos are loud,
They pat on he's back and they make him so proud,
They give him mezcal and the barbacue meat,
They tell him, "Amigo, we can't be defeat."
But efter elaction he no gotta fran',
The Mexico-Texan he no gotta lan',

Except for a few with their cunning and craft
He count just as much as a nought to the laft,
And they say everywhere, "He's a burden and drag,
He no gotta country, he no gotta flag."
He no gotta voice, all he got is the han'
To work like the burro; he no gotta lan'.

And only one way can his sorrows all drown,
He'll get drank as hell when next payday come roun',
For he has one advantage of all other man,
Though the Mexico-Texan he no gotta lan',

He can get him so drank that he think he will fly
Both September the Sixteen and Fourth of July.[15]

As a poet, Américo Paredes begins to explore the concept of what others outside the border culture think of the Mexico-Tejano people. Paredes uses the third person singular and plural, "he" and "they," to give an opinion of what he believes to be the Mexico-Texan's self-image of himself based on what others think of him. The poem is insightful because it suggests how an in-between existence muddles and yet shapes the Mexico-Texan's identity.

One of Américo Paredes's better poems that moves closer to the spirit and essence of the old ranching culture along the Lower Rio Grande border is "Guitarreros" (1935).[16] The poem begins with an epitaph from one of Américo Paredes's favorite corridos titled "El hijo desobediente." The folk song is about a young man who disobeys his father while in a fight. The boy curses his father by threatening to kill him if he interferes. Having made these comments, the boy knows he must suffer the consequences for his lack of respect. According to the corrido scholar Merle Simmons, a kind of divine punishment awaits him. The *castigo* (punishment) will manifest itself in the form of a violent death.[17] The boy, therefore, wishes to be buried anywhere but in sacred ground. The epitaph, *bajaron el toro prieto / que nunca habían bajado*, alludes to this violent death on the horns of an enraged bull. The didactic folk song reveals the respect one should have toward others, especially one's father. The theme of respect and honor is hinted at in the poem by the way in which singing was done in the old ranching culture. The poem suggests that few *guitarreros* are able to keep this tradition alive:

Guitarreros

bajaron el toro prieto,
que nunca lo habían bajado . . .

Black against twisted black
The old mesquite
Rears up against the stars
Branch bridle hanging,
While the bull comes down from the mountain
Driven along by your fingers,
Twenty nimble stallions prancing up and down
the *redil* of the guitars.

One leaning on the truck, one facing—
Now the song:
Not cleanly flanked, not pacing,
But in a stubborn yielding that unshapes
And shapes itself again,
Hard-mouthed, zigzagged, thrusting,
Thrown not sung
One to the other.
The old man listens in his cloud
Of white tobacco smoke.
"It was so," he says,
"In the old days it was so."[18]

A closer analysis of the poem's title suggests a tribute to the way in which folk poetry was performed in the old days. Images of the ranching life combine with those of lyrical music to offer a glimpse of a traditional performance—proud and dignified. The poetic voice offers a glimpse of the folk artists' attitudes toward some of the changes that have taken place along the Lower Rio Grande region. The moral order evoked by the corrido is senseless in a world were God no longer exists.[19]

Américo Paredes's dedication to his poetry helped him win the first-place award in a statewide high school poetry contest sponsored by Trinity College (now Trinity University in San Antonio, Texas). The poem, a sonnet entitled "Night," came to the attention of "Red" Irving, Paredes's high school principal who was also the dean of the local junior college at the time. After high school graduation, Irving noticed Paredes standing around a street corner looking for a job. The principal encouraged Paredes to apply for a student assistantship, even though the deadline had passed. Through Irving's effort Américo Paredes received a college work-study award that enabled him to pay for his college tuition at Brownsville Junior College.[20]

While attending junior college in the mid 1930s during the Great Depression, Américo Paredes worked long hours. In addition to his student assistantship, he worked approximately fifty hours a week at Cárdenas's Grocery Store for two dollars a week. In spite of his limited resources Américo continued to work at his craft in his spare time and at the age of twenty-two published his first volume of lyric poetry titled *Cantos de adolescencia* (1937). The poetic voice in this collection is that of a youngster in search of an identity that is neither Mexican nor American but Mexico-Tejano, as the prologue suggests.

> Los versos que en este libro se encierran no son solamente el "diario de un adolescente." Son el diario de un adolescente méxico-texano.
>
> ¡Adolescente! Fenómeno físico causado por la proximidad de dos edades; individuo que no es niño ni es adulto. ¡México-texano! Fenómeno sociológico, planta de tiesto, hombre sin terruño propio y verdadero, que no es ni mexicano ni yanqui.[21]

> The verses that are inside of this book are not only the "diary of an adolescent." It is the diary of a Mexico-Tejano adolescent!

> Adolescent! Physical phenomenon caused by the proximity of two ages; individual that is neither child nor adult. Mexico-Tejano! Sociological phenomenon, stubborn plant, man without his true and proper country, that is neither Mexican nor Yankee. (Author's translation)

If earlier the young Américo used the English language to convey his innermost feelings of exile, now he makes a conscious effort to articulate this search in his native tongue:

> Estas páginas son el resultado de esta lucha de tiempo de decisión. Comencé a escribir verso desde la edad de quince años pero mis obras fueron todas en inglés. Mis versos en español no comienzan hasta en 1932, dos años después. Esto se debe a la influencia de una escuela en inglés y de muy pocos libros en la lengua de Cervantes. En verdad, todavía me siento más seguro de mí mismo en la lengua de Shakespeare que en la mía. Por eso encontrará el lector en mis versos errores de gramática. Pero no crea él que están allí por falta de cuidado. La mayor parte fueron corregidos. Los que quedan fueron dejados al propósito, porque en mi concepto, no se pueden remover. Así—en aquellas palabras—"sentí" lo que quería decir. Decirlo de otra manera fuera no decirlo.[22]

> These pages are the result of this struggle in a time of decision. I began to write verse at the age of fifteen but all my work was in English. My Spanish verses do not begin until 1932, two years later. This is due to the influence of an English school and of very few books in the language of Cervantes. Indeed, I still feel myself more secure in the language of Shakespeare than in my own. That is why the

> reader will find in my verses grammatical errors. However, the reader should not believe that these errors are there due to carelessness. The majority of them were corrected. The ones that remained were left there on purpose because to my mind, they cannot be removed. That is how—in those words—"I felt" what I wanted to say. To say it another way would have been not to say it at all. (Author's translation)

The small book consists of sixty-two poems, divided into nine sections: "La lira patriótica" (The Patriotic Lyre), "La música" (The Music), "La naturaleza" (Nature), "La comedia del amor" (The Comedy of Love), "La tragedia del amor" (The Tragedy of Love), "In Memoriam," "La voz rebelde" (The Rebellious Voice), "Décimas" (Spanish stanzas in octosyllabic lines), and "L'envoi" (verses placed at the end of a ballad in praise of someone.) Although the poems in *Cantos de adolescencia* are generally weak in poetic style, they represent Américo Paredes's first attempt at Spanish verse.

The poem "México, La Ilusión del Continente" (Mexico, the Continent's Dream) is a good example of Américo's continued search for a distinct Chicano expression. Here, the poetic voice laments his in-between existence and mourns his southern country's condition; yet in spite of these circumstances the poet remains loyal to his native people and homeland as the final stanzas of the poem suggest.

México, La Ilusión del Continente

¡Audaz tribuno de las frases bellas!
cuando la pena o el dolor me hiera,
¡enséñame a ser águila altanera
para volar contigo a las estrellas!

Y si mi espíritu se encuentra yerto,
si un César me consigna en el Calvario,
¡hazme un nopal heróico y solitario
que crece entre las peñas del desierto!

Mi alma que en tinieblas fué indecisa
espera una palabra que la alienta;
quiere ser . . . ¡siquiera una serpiente
que hiere al presuntuoso que la pisa!

Será mi luz, la estrella que me guía,
el águila, el nopal y la serpiente:
¡México! ¡La ilusión del continente!
¡México! ¡La ilusión del alma mía!

Mexico, the Continent's Dream

Audacious tribune of beautiful phrases!
when shame and pain may hurt me
teach me to be a proud eagle
to fly with you to the stars!

And if my spirit finds itself dead,
if a Cesar assigns me to Calvary,
make me a lone and heroic cactus
that grows among the destitution of the desert!
My spirit that in darkness was indecisive
awaits a word that will inspire it
it wants to be . . . at least a serpent
that wounds the conceited that steps on it!

It shall be my light, the star that guides me,
the eagle, the cactus, and the serpent:

> Mexico! The dream of the continent!
> Mexico! The dream of my soul! (Author's translation)

Instead of spiritual worship, the poetic voice searches for guidance and inspiration from his motherland, and the eagle, cactus, and serpent (the images in the center of the Mexican flag) represent symbols of optimism, perseverance, and courage. The poet is proud of the fact that he is Mexican, even though he believes that his new country of the United States despises his native heritage.

Américo Paredes received his associate degree from Brownsville Junior College in 1936. He was unable to continue his education during the Depression because he could not afford it. He quit his grocery store job at Cárdenas's when he was hired as a proofreader and translator with the *Brownsville Herald.* The salary was the same, two dollars a week, but the new job gave him more time to read and write, and he learned to type. In time Américo Paredes became part of the regular staff at the *Brownsville Herald* where he proofread many articles by J. Frank Dobie, who wrote regularly for the newspaper. Paredes was often angered by the content of Dobie's articles with regard to the Mexican people; he felt that his tone was condescending.[23] Because Américo Paredes could not challenge Dobie's opinions in the newspaper, he channeled his anger and frustration into his own creative writings. He mocked J. Frank Dobie in his semiautobiographical novel *George Washington Gómez,* which he was writing at the time. Américo wrote candidly about what he really thought of the celebrated folklorist. "K. Hank Harvey . . . was considered the foremost of authorities on the Mexicans of Texas. . . . Harvey was a self-made man. After he had come to Texas, with only a few years of schooling, he resolved to become an authority on Texas history and folklore. In a few years he had read every book there was on the early history of Texas, it was said, and his fellow Texans accepted him as the historical oracle of the state.

There was a slight hitch, it is true. Most early Texas history books were written in Spanish, and K. Hank didn't know the language. However, nobody mentioned this, and it didn't detract from Harvey's glory."[24] Although the young Américo did not know Dobie as a person, he characterized him negatively in his book. According to Américo Paredes, J. Frank Dobie originated the word "wetback" (a name used to refer to Mexicans, especially illegals), and this infuriated Paredes.[25] He detested the negative stereotypes that many North Americans had toward his people.

Américo Paredes's Fictional Examples of Folklore as Performance

George Washington Gómez: A Mexicotexan Novel (1990) is Américo Paredes's best work completed during this period, although it was not published until fifty years later. The manuscript was sent to publishers, but the novel was controversial and no one wanted to publish it.[26] The novel is filled with information about Paredes's life in south Texas, as well as real-life figures, historical events, and traditional folk performances that transform the bildüngsroman into an important historical document. The novel re-creates the Mexican people's struggle in south Texas during an important period in U.S. history.[27] If history is an objective representation of an event, Américo Paredes exposed the limits of this discipline by anticipating what would happen as a result of the cultural and socioeconomic forces that shaped the lives of the Mexico-Tejano people. Aristotle's *Poetics* suggests that the combination of facts with highly probable events gives a story a potentiality more persuasive than an objective historical account.[28] *George Washington Gómez* is prophetic in that it foreshadows the fate of many Mexican Americans. Paredes understood that the North American socialization process of adolescents, achieved mostly through the English-speaking public educational system, affected the culture and identity of these Mexican people.

The young Américo documents some of the issues that preoccupied him, most notably the effects of a North American capitalist economy and the tension it created among the traditional ranching communities along the Lower Rio Grande border. Aside from the salient themes of cultural conflict and the search for a distinct Chicano perspective, Américo Paredes began to underscore the element of folklore as performance—the re-creation of songs, tales, and jests by verbal artists. But these expressive models often achieved another level of significance for Américo Paredes when outsiders became involved in the creative act. Two instances in *George Washington Gómez* reveal how a Mexican American identity may be performed for strategic reasons, usually to poke fun at people. In each case the border Mexican assumes a typical, negative stereotype of the Mexican, based in part on what he thinks the outsider thinks about him. The performer will use a masked identity to fool and outfox strangers, and Américo Paredes was sensitive to this sort of behavior. His literary approach to folklore as performance suggests a play with Mexican American identity to outwit people, especially those that conduct themselves arrogantly in the presence of such folk. For example, Vicente and Manuel are two characters in *George Washington Gómez* who serve as fictional pieces for Américo Paredes's idea of performance. In each case, the border Mexican plays with an identity to mock those who may consider the people along the Lower Rio Grande region to be stupid or inferior.

Vicente at the WOW Social Club exemplifies this type of creativity among the border folk though people outside the culture may perceive them differently. He is a bald, "deep-dark, roly-poly fellow" who sits and listens to an outsider's commentary about how things are better where he is from. Francisco, the teenage outsider, declares, "In Monterrey all the important men play pool. And they are very good. Man, this is nothing. You should see General Almazán play."[29] Although a Mexican, Francisco is not a border Mexican, and his loftiness bothers some of the individuals at the pool hall, including Vicente. As the teenager selects a cue, he brags about how he used to play pool with prominent military officials like General Almazán and how his grandfather Gen. Epifanio Sidar was once governor of Nuevo León.

> "I saw General Sidar once," said a man [Vicente] in the group of watchers. "He was riding a white horse. *¡Lindo Penco!*" He shook his round, recently-shaven head, as if the remembered beauty of the general's horse were a tragic thing.
>
> "You knew my grandfather? Do you remember the flight toward the border in 1913?"
>
> "No," the man said, his pouchy, heavy-lidden eyes very sad. "I was here in Texas then."[30]

Having lost his game of pool, Francisco continues his tale when he realizes that his group of watchers have become listeners, too. The teenager chooses Vicente, the bald gentleman in a blue shirt and overalls, as his main target. The border Mexican then plays a stereotypical role. "He sat on the bench, hands between his legs, grasping the bench and looking up at Francisco in a parody of the humble attention that the Mexican *peón* used to give the *hacendado*."[31] The group listens for quite some time to Francisco's narrative about his famous grandfather, General Sidar, and later about the skill of a baseball pitcher who failed to make the major leagues because he never came to the United States. According to the Mexican teen, the pitcher could make a ball drop straight down in front of the plate to the amazement of everyone.

> "Aw" said the tableboy, "that's too green. It doesn't freeze at all. Pitching a ball that drops straight down just in front of the plate!"
>
> Francisco gave the boy a superior smile. "You don't understand what skill can do," he said.
>
> "That's true," said Vicente, the man who remembered the general's white horse. "Skill can do wonderful things. I remember a man I knew up above in North Texas. He was very skilled with his hands. Owned a fighting cock that was the best in the region. Had never lost a fight.
>
> "But one day he met his match." Vicente's eyes softened in reminiscence. "What fight! My friend took his rooster out before the other bird killed him, but he was an awfully battered bird. His right leg was so torn up it had to be cut off. But did my friend wring the cock's neck? No. Do you know what he did? He cut off the bad leg, very carefully, and sewed up the skin up very fine. Then came the real wonder. He took a piece of wood and whittled and whittled till he made a perfect rooster's leg, down to the spur and the toe-nails."[32]

Vicente continues to tell Francisco about the fighting cock with the wooden leg, but that was not the end of the story, only half of it. According to the border Mexican, the rooster later lost his left wing in another fight, and the owner decided to make his bird a "'wing out of thin leather. He went to work and made a framework out of stiff wire and on this he fastened the leather cover, with a lot of care. He was a skillful man. He painted feathers on the leather wing and made it look a lot like a real one. He strapped this wing on the stump of the real one. And he did it so well the rooster could flap it and use it just as if it had been grown there. It was a sight to see that bird going after the hens with his leather wing stretched out over the ground.' Vicente stopped and nodded slowly, as if mourning his friend's wasted talents."[33] Francisco, amazed by the story, asks impatiently what happened next. And Vicente solemnly adds: "Why . . . after that the cock never lost a fight. He'd just lead with his leather wing and knock them out with his wooden leg."[34] At these outrageous and patently false statements, everyone laughs aloud except Vicente, who exacerbates Francisco's humiliation by adopting a perplexed appearance at all the merriment. Francisco, unaware of border Mexican folklore, has been the target of Vicente's practical joke.

The story of the gamecock, its performance, and the audience's reception of the anecdote in *George Washington Gómez* offers an early glimpse of Américo Paredes's vision of folklore. He believed that careful attention needed to be given to the performers, their performance, and the context of the performance to fully appreciate the dynamics of folklore. In this case, Vicente's story and performance is a reaction to Francisco's arrogance at the pool hall. The border Mexican simply went along with the Mexican's attitude about how things were done much better in Monterrey, Mexico, to call attention to Francisco's bravado.

Guálinto "George" Gómez, the protagonist in *George Washington Gómez,* becomes the subject of criticism, too, for his arrogance. Despite being born and raised among the border folk, Guálinto left the area to get a college education and is now a first lieutenant in counterintelligence for the U.S. Army. With the onset of WWII, he makes an infrequent visit to his hometown of San Pedrito with his wife, Ellen Dell, a blond, blue-eyed professional and the daughter of a former Texas Ranger. His family and friends notice the changes in Guálinto, but the young Mexican American lieutenant does not care about their views. George is convinced that his new adopted cultural values are more important than his Mexican traditions, even though in his dreams he is often at war with himself and his people's past.[35] In his eagerness to obtain complete assimilation into North American society, the young Mexican American experiences internal conflicts and feelings of inferiority. George Gómez believes that he is better than his people, and a visit to his old barber shop exemplifies this change in attitude. "He had always enjoyed getting a haircut. The precise, unhurried sound of the barber's shears. The ever-exploring comb, the almost imperceptible tug of the busy scissors. They caused a gentle, pleasant tingle to the scalp. A caress. He liked the barber's massaging, the comb's teeth through his hair, and the light scraping of metal against the back of his neck. It relaxed him, and he felt at peace with the world. Often he had wondered if dogs felt like this when they had their ears scratched. But dogs did not have to put up with barber shop conversation."[36] Some of the men at the barbershop recognize Guálinto's aloofness, and so one of them, Manuel, assumes the role of the dumb Mexican in a conversation about the weather, while the other border Mexicans play along. Leytón, González, and Manuel agree that it was much cooler in the old days.

> "If we are to believe the newspapers and the salesmen, we have a wonderful climate," Manuel said indignantly. "But it's hot enough in this town. It was cooler twenty years ago, but now? Whew!"
>
> "Maybe it's because of the pavements and all the new buildings," González suggested.
>
> "Pavements nothing!" Manuel, said, "It's the lack of air, that's what. Twenty years ago there were no automobiles to speak of, and there was a lot of air. Now all the air is stored in these gasoline stations so they can fill the tires of all these automobiles. We don't have enough air left to breathe cool."[37]

After his haircut, George later contemplates Manuel's remarks on his way to his uncle's farm. The first lieutenant in counterintelligence questions whether the old man and the others were joking or not since "Manuel was stupid enough to believe what he had said about the lack of air" and besides "they were all a bunch of dum-dums."[38] It appears that George's separation from his Mexican culture distorts his perception of his people. He can no longer determine whether the border folk's small talk is banter or ignorance. That is, in his desire to achieve full acceptance into North American society, he has accepted stereotypical views about border Mexicans. Don Manuel may have thought that George believed he was too good for his own people with his lofty attitude. The old man, thus, turned the conversation into a folk performance to mock the young Mexican American for his aloofness at the barbershop.

Américo Paredes's Experiences with Journalism, Marriage, and WWII

While at the *Brownsville Herald* Américo Paredes met Hart Stilwell, and the two became friends. Stilwell used Américo as a resource person for his novel titled *Border City* (1945)—a book about the racial conflict between Anglos and Mexicans along the Lower Rio Grande border. Although Hart Stilwell makes the novelist's usual claim that the characters are fictitious and "any resemblance to any person, living or dead, is purely coincidental," one might well wonder if Pepe, a young Mexican American with fair skin, gray green eyes, who "could have passed for pure Spaniard," is Américo Paredes.[39] If so, certain passages in the story offer insight to some of Paredes's opinions with regard to Christianity and the Mexican people's socioeconomic situation. For example, an interesting characteristic of Pepe is his anticlerical views, and he is often upset by Mexicans' lack of political activism due to their religious devotion. When Chelo Moreno gives a crucifix as a gift to Dave Atwood for his assistance, the Anglo newspaperman is moved by her faith and gesture. Dave then shows the cross to his friend and coworker, Pepe, who is not impressed. The editor of the Spanish edition of the newspaper bitterly replies: "Don't let it move you too far. . . . It has helped to move my own people into a condition of slavery and keep them there for three hundred years. . . . For three hundred years and more—yes, for two thousand years—those who rule have used the Catholic Church to keep the poor people poor, to keep the ignorant people ignorant, to fill them with nameless fears and blind them to reason when they are little children so that they can be herded and driven and worked until they drop dead of exhaustion; still they are afraid to cry out. Show me no crosses, my friend. No crosses."[40] These views expressed by Pepe are in line with Américo Paredes's belief with regard to the role of the Catholic Church. He was very anticlerical and usually attended church only for baptisms, weddings, and funerals.[41] Paredes believed the Catholic Church was too conservative and failed to address the injustices and racism Mexicans endured in south Texas.

In Brownsville, Américo Paredes met Consuelo "Chelo" Silva, a well-known vocalist in the Lower Rio Grande region and a native of Brownsville, Texas. Américo fell in love with her, and he composed and sang his songs to her. Soon, Américo and Chelo were performing traditional music for weddings and parties, and at a local Brownsville radio station before World War II. The couple married in 1939 and had a son, Américo Paredes Jr. But the marriage did not last. After the couple divorced, Chelo Silva went on to become a celebrated singer throughout Greater Mexico and South America.

Américo obtained a government job with Pan American Airways in 1940, where he inspected fighter jet planes sent to Europe during World War II. This government job exempted him from being drafted into the U.S. Army. He kept his job with the *Brownsville Herald* on weekends, and he continued playing on the radio in the evenings. This was not a high point in his life, especially after his divorce from Chelo Silva. He wanted to get away from the area and felt guilty because his two younger brothers, Amador and Eleazar, and many of his close friends were overseas fighting in World War II. Like many other Mexicans in the United States, Américo did not consider himself an "American" but rather a Mexican living in the United States. Nonetheless, he decided to quit his job with Pan American and volunteer for military service. In August 1944, Américo Paredes enlisted in the U.S. Army.

He was stationed in Japan and within a month, World War II was over. He chose to remain in Japan where he worked as a journalist for *Pacific Stars and Stripes*, the newspaper of the U.S. Army. He later was offered the post of political editor for *Pacific Stars and Stripes* and began to cover the war crime trials and other issues of political interest.[42] The exposure to the court system and due process would later inform his book *"With His Pistol in His Hand"* (1958). Américo's work with newspaper reports, official documents, letters, and interviews concerning the criminal cases against Japanese officials would help him tremendously with his own scholarly research.[43]

From the Far East, he also wrote articles in Spanish for Mexico City's *Universal*. These weekly articles consisted of sketches about life in China, Korea, and Japan. As a novice anthropologist Américo Paredes began to study the clash of cultures in other parts of the world. As early as 1947 Paredes began to write about North American expansionism and its effects.

Todo Tokio tiene cierto aire norteamericano. Las calles lucen letreros en inglés y además tienen nombres ahora, o más bien números e iniciales al estilo poco imaginativo de los militares. En las calles se ven autos acabados de recibir de Estados Unidos por los trabajadores que se encuentran en Tokio. En los distritos residenciales hay letreros frente a las residencias, los cuales nos dicen que aquí vive el coronel fulano y acá el general zutano del ejército yanqui. En el centro de la ciudad hay una enorme tienda para el personal de la ocupación, donde se encuentra cualquier cosa, desde pañuelos y jugo de tomate hasta una barbería y un restaurante. Hay más teatros y hay que pagar para entrar, cosa que no era hace seis meses—hay más lugares donde comer. Y hay más distancia entre la población japonesa y la nueva población de Tokio que antiguamente entre los japoneses y los primeros soldados norteamericanos.[44]

All of Tokyo has a North American air. The streets have lighted signs in English and they now have names too, or better still numbers and initials in a style with little imagination from the military. In the streets one sees cars recently received from the United States for workers who are found in Tokyo. In the residential districts there are signs in front of the home, the ones that inform us that colonel so-and-so lives here and over here general so-and-so from the Yankee military. In downtown there is a huge store for the military personnel where everything is found from handkerchiefs to tomato juice, even a barbershop and restaurant. There are more theaters and one now has to pay to enter, something that was not done six months ago—there are more places to eat. And there is more of

> a distance between the Japanese population and the new population of Tokyo than before between the Japanese and the first North American soldiers. (Author's translation)

Américo was interested in the acculturation process of the Japanese society where men, women, and children would soon begin to learn English and the American way of life—much like what happened in the Lower Rio Grande region. He expressed compassion in his article toward the defeated Japanese people who would experience a different life under the influence and occupation of the United States.

In 1946 *Pacific Stars and Stripes* reduced its personnel, and Américo Paredes was discharged from active duty. (It was around this time that he met one of his dearest friends, Horst de la Croix; the two would share a friendship for more that thirty years.) He then took a job as a public relations officer for the American Red Cross in China. In connection with this position, Paredes witnessed much destruction, poverty, and emotional suffering caused by the war, especially in Korea. In 1948 when the Communists began to make advances in China, the Red Cross recalled its personnel and Paredes was again unemployed. He returned to Japan and became the editor of a small weekly army journal intended for the American troops stationed in Japan.

While in Japan Américo Paredes met and married his second wife, Amelia Shidzu Nagamine, on May 28, 1948. He enrolled in English and American literature through the correspondence program at the University of Texas at Austin. He had access to the library of the U.S. Armed Forces College, known among the troops as Tokyo College. Paredes borrowed many books from Tokyo College. He discovered several major writers including William Faulkner. In July 1950, Américo and Amelia Paredes left Japan and returned to the United States so he could pursue his literary studies.

Amelia was the daughter of a Japanese father and a Uruguayan mother. Because of her Japanese background, she was not allowed to enter the United States as a permanent resident.[45] She obtained a visa for six months with the option of renewing it for a maximum of another six months. The couple went to live in Matamoros, Tamaulipas, Mexico, with one of Américo's brothers for two months and moved to Austin, Texas, in September. Soon after relocating, Américo and Amelia became parents. Alan Paredes was born on July 13, 1951.

A Maverick at the University of Texas at Austin

At the age of thirty-five, Américo planned to complete his bachelor's degree in a year at the University of Texas at Austin and then move to northern Mexico where he had relatives and where there was less prejudice against Asians. He carried a full load of courses that emphasized writing and literary criticism. Amelia helped him by assuming the majority of the household responsibilities, which allowed her husband to devote himself to his studies. Américo Paredes earned a bachelor of arts degree, summa cum laude, in English and Philosophy in 1951. Fortunately, during the year, the immigration law was amended and Amelia received permanent residence. The faculty encouraged Américo to work on a graduate degree in English and the couple decided to stay in Austin.

Américo Paredes participated in several literary competitions as a way to make extra income for the family. He received the first-place prize of the *Dallas Times Herald* short-story writing contest with a collection of short stories titled *Border Country* (1952). The prize consisted of five hundred dollars worth of books. Paredes later won another first-place prize in the D. A. Frank novel writing contest with his short book *The Shadow* (1998). This time, however, the award was five hundred dollars, and according to Paredes, "it was a welcome boost to the family bank account and to [his] ego as well."[46]

Américo modified his course of study in graduate school to emphasize folklore. While comparing two versions of a Scottish ballad "Sir Patrick Spens," Américo Paredes remembered his childhood days when the old men gathered in the evenings along the border. He recalled the importance of context and performance in the interpretation of songs and legends. The mood of the group played a fundamental role in the narration of the ballad and story. He brought something on the corrido to his professor of literary criticism, who then referred him to another professor, Robert Stephenson. As a professor in English and Spanish, Stephenson also taught courses in folklore, and Paredes talked to him about the corrido of Gregorio Cortez. The two conversed for a time and Américo changed his course of study to folklore for his master's and Ph.D. Since his subject was balladry, the English department required him to take courses in medieval balladry and on Shakespeare, Chaucer, and the history of the English language. Paredes also had to take a number of courses in the Spanish department, including ones on *El Cid*, the history of the Spanish language, and *el siglo de oro*. In his study of English and Scottish ballads, he read the works of Francis James Child, Helen Child Sargent, and George Lyman Kittredge; and in Spanish balladry, Ramón Menéndez Pidal, Ramón Meléndez Pelayo, and Vicente Mendoza. The education he received was liberal, not resembling a typical scholar's focus on one particular subject. His personal library included fiction, history, anthropology, and folklore. This learning complemented his oral traditional development with the border folk.

In his study of folklore Américo Paredes received the assistance of Stith Thompson, one of the most highly regarded folklore scholars in the United States and Europe. A visiting professor at the time, Thompson became a member of Paredes's dissertation committee. Thompson was impressed by Paredes's dissertation, "'El Corrido de Gregorio Cortez': A Ballad of Border Conflict" (1956), and recommended it for publication by the University of Texas Press. The English department wanted him to stay, but the administration had a policy against hiring their own graduates and also preferred to hire younger professors.[47] Américo Paredes was forty-one years old and had all three of his degrees from UT. To get around the policy of not hiring its own graduates, the English department arranged for him to teach for a year at Texas Western College (now the University of Texas, El Paso), a branch of UT. While there, Américo received a call from the director of the UT Press, informing him that they had a copy of his manuscript. The director planned to publish it, but wanted Paredes to moderate his comments about Walter Prescott Webb, Texas' renowned historian, and the Texas Rangers.[48] Paredes refused and asked the director to return the manuscript. Fearing that Américo Paredes might publish it somewhere else, the University of Texas Press decided to publish a revised form of his dissertation. The chapter on the rise and fall of the Mexican corrido was omitted.

After a year at Texas Western, Américo returned to the English department at UT as a visiting faculty member to teach courses in American literature, creative writing, and folklore. In 1958 the University of Texas Press published *"With His Pistol in His Hand": A Border Ballad and Its Hero*, and UT hired him as an assistant professor. The Press customarily had a signing party after a book was published. But because relations between author and Press had been strained by Paredes's refusal to moderate his comments about the Texas Rangers and Walter Prescott Webb no such event was held. According to Paredes, after the book was published, a retired Texas Ranger visited the director of the Press and demanded to know where the author was so he could "pistol whip him" for his comments about the Texas Rangers.[49] But the Press said such information was confidential. Aside from this incident, Paredes's book on border culture received little recognition after its initial publication.

Américo and Amelia had their second son, Vicente, on January 9, 1955, and a daughter, Julia (Julie), was born on October 23, 1959. Everything seemed to be going fine for the Paredes family. They had made many good friends in Austin, and Américo was building up a fine reputation as a folklorist and scholar.[50] He was asked "to give lectures at other campuses, to appear on TV programs to talk about folklore," and to sing and play guitar.[51] In 1961 the family bought their first home and their first car, and the University of West Virginia hired him for the summer to give a lecture on Latin American culture. The Paredes family had the opportunity to travel and visit places like Morgantown, Niagara Falls, Washington, D.C., and the Smoky Mountains. But this was perhaps "the last time [they had] been really happy as a family."[52] Julie seemed withdrawn and was not talking at twenty-two months. Amelia knew something was wrong and the couple visited hospitals and clinics as far as Michigan, to discover what was wrong with Julie. A group of neurologists informed the psychiatrists that it was brain damage and not mental retardation. The family had been in an automobile accident when Amelia was five months pregnant, and neurologists concluded that this was the probable cause.[53] It was a difficult time, and initially the couple blamed themselves for their daughter's condition. Julie underwent physical therapy at home, seven days a week, in efforts to improve her mental state. Amelia assumed most of the responsibility for the care and safety of Julie, although Américo gave what time he could in the mornings and evenings, and on weekends. These were difficult times for the whole family.

In addition to his teaching responsibilities at UT, Américo Paredes was in charge of the folklore archive in the English department. As organizer and director, Américo Paredes began to collaborate with the anthropology department to prepare a folklore curriculum. Although the Texas Folklore Society continued to function as an adjunct to the English department, Paredes wanted to break free in order to create a center for folklore studies and to distance himself from what he considered "the WASP-dominated Old Guard."[54] He felt that his Texas predecessor's approach to folklore was romantic and condescending, especially toward Mexicans. Even though he attended their regular meetings, he was convinced that these reunions were pretty much "literary entertainments" rather than scholarship. In 1961 when Roger D. Abrahams, who would become a renowned folklorist, delivered a theoretical paper at one of their meetings ("The Changing Concept of the Negro Hero"), the TFS members responded to his talk with open sarcasm. They thought Roger D. Abrahams' presentation was not folklore because it was too abstract.[55] These ideological differences between the old and new folklorists continued in the English department. Under the supervision of an interdisciplinary folklore program committee, of which he was a member, Paredes was an early contributor to a cultural studies approach with his cross-disciplinary perspective. But at the time the chair of the department, Mody C. Boatright, saw no need to formalize a separate program for folklore studies. The chair of the English department declared that he did not "advocate any change in [the] program, even though [he was] aware that meeting degree requirements in the departments leaves the student too little time for the mastery of folklore."[56]

Frustrated with the lack of support, Paredes began to look for work elsewhere until Rick Adams, chair of the anthropology department, offered him a part-time appointment in 1966. The new position supported the work Américo had begun at the folklore archive and the development of a folklore curriculum. With the help of members from several academic departments, the Center for Intercultural Studies in Folklore and Oral History was established in 1967. Mody C. Boatright was named as founding director; Américo Paredes was named director of the center the following year. Paredes was steadfast in his efforts to separate physically and ideologically from the Texas Folklore Society, and in 1968 he initiated the interdisciplinary graduate folklore major in the English and anthropology departments. Richard Bauman, who would become another highly influential social scientist, joined the anthropology department in 1968, and Roger D. Abrahams would divide his time between the English and anthropology departments as well. The new trio of scholars, Paredes, Abrahams, and Bauman, soon "energized the broader interest in performance that flowered at the University of Texas in the late '60s through the mid-'80s."[57]

But Paredes's frustrations continued at the University of Texas at Austin in spite of his leadership and his contributions as a scholar. The Chicano movement was in full swing throughout the American Southwest, and Américo Paredes demonstrated his activism not only in theory but in practice. Chicana and Chicano student activists petitioned for the creation of a Mexican American studies program, and the university responded with the organization of an ad hoc faculty council committee on May 20, 1969, to ensure the formation of such a program. Américo Paredes was named director of the operation (1970–72), and he immediately began to organize an independent Mexican American studies degree separate from an already existing "ethnic studies" major. The curriculum proposal was approved by the university's committee on degrees and courses, although successive administrations time and time again prevented the official implementation of the program. The university's explanation was that the delays were the result of a "mistake," "a breakdown in communication," and an "administrative error."[58] Between 1970 and 1972 Américo Paredes resigned twice as director of the Mexican American studies program, but both times he returned because of his commitment to his students. He was convinced that the University of Texas at Austin did not support a genuine and meaningful Mexican American studies program and that it was content with a mediocre "ethnic studies" major. In a letter published on February 3, 1972, by the *Daily Texan* (the campus newspaper), Américo Paredes explained his decision to be relieved for a third time as director of the program, and he expressed his attitude toward the concept of "ethnic studies" versus studies focused on a particular ethnic group.

> Perhaps I should explain my position about "ethnic studies." I support the teaching of ethnic studies courses within departments. I am strongly opposed, however, to degree programs built upon a general concept of ethnicity. Such "ethnic studies" programs can too easily become a "lands-and-peoples" sort a thing, not quite as broadening as a ten-days' trip around the world. The "look-we-are-all-ethnics" approach may be valid for the primary grades, but it is highly questionable at the university level.
>
> It is a different matter when a program brings together materials and methods from different disciplines and focuses them on one specific ethnic group. This approach, to my mind, justifies its reason for existence because of its fresh viewpoints into education, and because it can organize new knowledge that may be brought to bear on minority problems within our society. Only two programs of this kind make sense in the State of Texas, Black Studies and Chicano Studies.[59]

The administration eventually agreed to implement the Mexican American studies program and later a graduate program. Américo Paredes, once more, demonstrated his leadership as an intellectual with his cross-border or transnational approach toward this area of specialization. Today, the Center for Mexican American Studies (CMAS) is one of the top ethnic-study centers in the nation with some "thirty associated faculty who teach approximately sixty classes in Mexican American studies each year."[60] Américo Paredes was able to establish the Center for Mexican American Studies at the University of Texas at Austin with the collaboration and support of students, staff, and faculty such as the renowned George I. Sánchez. And like the Center for Intercultural Studies in Folklore and Oral History, the Center for Mexican American Studies has earned an outstanding reputation as one of the finest interdisciplinary schools in Chicana and Chicano cultural studies in the country. Many of Paredes's students have gone on to have distinguished careers.

Américo Paredes had a profound influence both within and beyond the academy. He received the respectful name of Don Américo, and many scholars recognize him as the "dean of Chicano studies" for being at the forefront in the analysis, interpretation, and understanding of Mexican American culture.[61] As a scholar and musician, he became a kind of a folk hero for many people because he was willing to stand up for the poor and underprivileged. His activities and his person are in line with what Edward E. Said in his book *Representations of the Intellectual* (1994) considers to be the role of the public intellectual. The Mexico-Tejano scholar was constantly "unmasking" the truth about Mexican stereotypes and was more than willing to speak about it in circles of power.[62] He was not afraid to stand up for his people. Américo Paredes was endowed with that special ability to embody an attitude and philosophy for a new generation of young scholars that believed in a better tomorrow. This was an ideal that he persistently worked for at the institution.

He would edit, translate, or write well over a hundred articles and reviews, as well as thirteen books on Mexican and Latino folklore and culture. In addition to his scholarly works, his poetry, short stories, and novels have been published. Américo Paredes also earned numerous formal distinctions such as a Guggenheim fellowship in 1962 for the collection of Mexican American folklore material, the first endowed professorship in his discipline in 1983, an annual lecture series since 1987 named in his honor, the Charles Frankel Award from the National Endowment for the Humanities in 1989 for giving general audiences a greater understanding of the humanities, and the Order of the Aztec Eagle (Aguila Azteca) in 1991, the highest distinction given by Mexico to foreign nationals who have made outstanding contributions to the improvement and extension of the values promoted by the government of Mexico. In 1997 the American Folklore Society recognized him as the most important scholar in the field of Mexican American folklore; in 1998 he was awarded a Lifetime Achievement Award at the state capitol during the opening session for the Texas Book Festival; and the Austin Independent School District named a new middle school after Paredes the same year. Among the scholarly groups bestowing honors upon him were the American Folklore Society, the North American Academy of the Spanish Language, the Sociedad Folklórica de México, and the Western Literature Association.

While at the University of Texas at Austin, he was often at political odds with the administration. He taught most of his classes in basements for twenty-five years and remained one of the lowest paid professors at UT for almost his entire career.[63] In 1984 when his younger brother, Amador, passed away Américo's health began to decline, forcing him into temporary retirement. Amador had suffered a slow and agonizing death from cancer, and Paredes became clinically depressed.[64] A few years later Américo Paredes was also diagnosed with cancer, although he continued to teach, make public appearances, and correspond with many of his former students and friends. He also made an effort to meet socially every Tuesday with Frances Terry, his former secretary and friend of thirty-one years, and he continued to be of service to the community until his very last days. "My heart will give out before the cancer gets me," Paredes once declared in a local Texas newspaper.[65] And that his how his life ended—*el cinco de mayo de* 1999. Américo Paredes died of pneumonia at Specialty Hospital in Austin, Texas. He was eighty-three years old. The keeper of the flame had been called home, leaving behind a legacy of the highest standards for others to follow.

The news of Américo Paredes's death spread throughout the United States and Mexico, casting a shadow over all those who had come to know him and his work. Many of his former students, colleagues, and friends remembered him with fond and inspiring memories. "The effect he had on his students was hypnotic," said Anthony N. Zavaleta, vice president for external affairs at the University of Texas at Austin. "He was, and in a way still is, one of the biggest, most influential figures in my life and not just in my academic life," Zavaleta stated.[66] José E. Limón, director of the Center for Mexican American Studies at the University of Texas at Austin, said that Américo Paredes "became . . . a kind of a living symbol of rectitude; of what is correct; of consummate integrity. He was an example for the way that men and women ought to conduct themselves in public and in private."[67] And Beverly J. Stoeltje, associate professor of folklore and communication and culture at Indiana University, Bloomington, declared that Paredes's "voice expressed his passion in every class, presentation, and song. His presence constituted a mark of integrity that could not be ignored. The linked pair, integrity and inspiration, will be forever associated with Don Américo."[68]

Américo Paredes's name and contributions still resonate today for many scholars, and to continue his remarkable story the following chapter examines the book that launched his career into legendary status, a study that exploded Texas history and the myth of the Texas Rangers, and one that revolutionized the study of cultures in south Texas. It is his most celebrated work, which in 2004 was in its fourteenth printing.

Américo's parents, Justo Paredes and Clotilde Manzano, in about 1914.

Américo with his sister Blanca. The photograph was taken in Brownsville, Texas, when Américo was approximately five years old. Notice Américo's melancholic expression.

Américo at Camp Robinson, Arkansas, in 1945, when he was twenty-nine. The photograph was for his mother.

Américo practicing his guitar outside his home in Brownsville, Texas, in the early 1930s. He was born in that house on September 15, 1915.

Américo in Tokyo in 1946. Army officers do not customarily squat for photographs, but Chicanos, particularly boys and young men, do. Obviously, this is a photograph of a U.S. officer overseas, Chicano style.

Amelia Shidzu Nagamine and Américo Paredes in Tokyo in 1948. The two are very much in love, and their marriage of more than fifty years was a special one.

Américo celebrates his thirty-third birthday in Tokyo. *Left to right:* His father-in-law, Naoya Honda Nagamine; his wife, Amelia Shidzu Paredes; Américo; his mother-in-law, María Julia Nagamine; and one of his best friends in the U.S. Army and back home in the states, Horst de la Croix.

In Brownsville, Texas, 1958, Américo Paredes discusses the publication of his book *"With His Pistol in His Hand": A Border Ballad and Its Hero*, with a radio presenter from station XEO. *"With His Pistol in His Hand,"* now in its fourteenth printing (2004), became his most famous work.

Top: Américo as a professor at the University of Texas at Austin in the 1970s. He is lecturing on Spanish balladry, such as the *romance*, *décima*, and *corrido*, of the Lower Rio Grande region. Paredes, an accomplished musician, played his guitar in the classroom for instructional purposes.

Right: Américo Paredes, professor emeritus of English and anthropology, in his late seventies. Many scholars regarded him as the "dean of Chicano studies."

Chapter 3

"With His Pistol in His Hand"

"I wonder what this Gringo thinks,"
Román said to himself. "He takes me for a fool.
But I'm going to make him such a trade that
he will remember me forever."
"With His Pistol in His Hand"—Américo Paredes

Américo Paredes discovered what could be considered a distinct Chicano perspective—in terms of literary style and content—with "el corrido de Gregorio Cortez," a ballad of border conflict. The Mexico-Tejano performer and scholar merged a Mexican oral legacy with a Protestant Anglo-Saxon literary tradition to challenge the conventional interpretations of Mexican Americans. *"With His Pistol in His Hand": A Border Ballad and Its Hero* celebrated the Mexican vaquero way of life and demonstrated how Texas culture was permeated with Mexican influences—a truth seldom acknowledged by North American scholars. He disputed the long-held belief that Mexican American culture was a bastardized mix of Anglo and Mexican influences and suggested that border culture was unique unto itself and contributed to both cultures. The idea was pioneering for its time, and the book became the fundamental text for Américo Paredes and the groundwork for the development of Chicano cultural studies.

A Hybrid Book and Then Some

"With His Pistol in His Hand" is a difficult text to pigeonhole because it is a hybrid of genres. The book is part history—in its discussion of the old Spanish province of Nuevo Santander in 1749; part folklore—in its study of oral tradition; part fiction—in its recreation of a story; part sociolinguistics—in its analysis of English words used in Spanish; part anthropology—in its ethnographic description of a culture; and part ethnomusicology—in its examination of the corrido (narrative folk song). The text erases or blurs the boundaries of any specialized subject and can be classified as postmodern with its use of newspapers, court documents, folk songs, and oral tradition. Paredes's self-reflexive study consists of two parts: book one, "Gregorio Cortez, the Legend and the Life," is an analysis of the sociopolitical climate and narrative nature of the historical event, and book two, "El Corrido de Gregorio Cortez, a Ballad of Border Conflict," serves as its scholarly complement, identifying the border corrido variants and presenting a theory of the genesis and supposed decline of this type of folk music along the Lower Rio Grande border.

In terms of historical, aesthetic, and theoretical perspectives, *"With His Pistol in His Hand"* has received the most attention by scholars and is considered the most influential book in Chicana and Chicano cultural studies.[1] Some critics examined Paredes's use of folklore to counteract the biased discourses established in Texas; another explained how Paredes's style of writing anticipated some of the trends in anthropology's "experimental moment"; while still another focused on Paredes's innovative stance as an ethnographer who transcribed and translated a group's storytelling performance. A few of the best-known critics are Ramón and José David Saldívar, José E. Limón, Renato Rosaldo, and Héctor Calderón. These scholars agree as to the impact Américo Paredes's book had in the evolution of Mexican American studies and in some cases on their own lives. I seek to add to their important contributions by examining Américo Paredes's idea of folklore as performance as another way to read "*With His Pistol in His Hand.*"

An Overview of His Most Famous Book

The book opens with a historical summary of José de Escandón's colonization efforts along the Lower Rio Grande region. These colonization tactics were different from other Spanish colonizers. Escandón did not use the Spanish presidio; his method involved a combination of settled families from the surrounding areas with newer ones from Querétaro. Incentives for the new settlers included freedom and autonomy from the officials of New Spain. The governor of Nuevo Santander delegated authority to his captains who, in turn, were responsible for the development and welfare of their own communities. The pastoral way of life organized in its socioeconomic base by the rancho and in its ideology by the ideals of Spanish chivalry fostered an informal culture and a natural equality among the men. By 1755 small ranching towns such as Camargo (1749), Guerrero (1750), Laredo (1755), Mier (1753), and Reynosa (1749) had been established along the river, and by 1835, an autonomous mestizo culture was beginning to develop when U.S. expansionism interrupted its progress.[2]

The history of the region is important if one is to understand the Rio Grande people. Border culture was informal and traditional, and the people did not write books to preserve their lifestyle. Themes about love, conflict, and rivalry were related through the spoken word, and if a local event was extraordinary, a folk poet sang about it to the people.[3] As an insider, Paredes juxtaposed the Mexican oral legacy with that of the Texas legend to distinguish between them. The latter did not belong to a people one would classify as "folk." The popular lore of the Anglo-Texan was circulated and supported by the literate and educated in books, magazines, and newspapers. Américo Paredes's collection, classification, and analysis of folklore from both groups told a different story from what was written in early Texas history. His interpretation revealed inconsistencies in the Anglo-Texan legend, proving that it was a fabrication. His interpretation of race relations between North Americans and Mexicans examined the issue of U.S. expansionism. "The truth seems to be that the old war propaganda concerning the Alamo, Goliad, and Mier later provided a convenient justification for outrages committed on the border by Texans of certain types, so convenient an excuse that it was artificially prolonged for almost a century. And had the Alamo, Goliad, and Mier not existed, they would have been invented as indeed they seem to have been in part."[4] Paredes felt that certain Texas intellectuals (like Walter Prescott Webb and J. Frank Dobie) used a discourse of propaganda to justify a war of expansionism against the Mexico-Tejano people. Américo Paredes wrote a moral history with the colonization efforts of the North American in mind. He questioned the motives and apparent justification for the demise of the Mexico-Tejanos in south Texas. If the war against Mexico was waged under the guise of Manifest Destiny, the battles in Texas served as a pretext for the dispossession of Mexico-Tejanos. Bribery, theft, and violence slowly displaced the Mexico-Tejanos from their lands.[5]

In view of the political and social climate of the Lower Rio Grande region, Paredes turned his attention to the oral traditions of the people. Chapter 2, "The Legend," is a replica of "an idealized, formal version of the legend," that takes place after a traditional performance of a corrido.[6] Paredes's re-created storytelling performance describes the fate of Gregorio Cortez, a border Mexican who kills Sheriff W. T. Morris on June 12, 1901, in Karnes County, Texas. Morris—a former Texas Ranger—and his deputy, Ben Choate, arrive at the Cortez residence to investigate a possible horse theft. Neither Morris nor Choate speaks Spanish fluently, and a misunderstanding sparks the conflict. Apparently, Choate translated Gregorio's remarks, which included the words *arrestar* (to arrest) and *nada* (nothing), to Sheriff Morris as "no white man can arrest me."[7] In a matter of seconds, Gregorio's brother, Román, and Sheriff Morris lie on the ground, each seriously wounded. Gregorio's remarks about the horse theft, as translated by Choate, caused Sheriff Morris to arrest Gregorio Cortez. Román attempts to tackle Morris, and the sheriff shoots him through the mouth. He then tries to kill Gregorio Cortez but misses despite being at close range. Gregorio grabs his gun from the back of his trousers and shoots Morris several times. Ben Choate runs for help, and Cortez flees the scene.

Cortez eludes various posses and kills another sheriff, Robert M. Glover. He travels some five hundred miles in a matter of days before Texas authorities arrest him. Cortez turns himself in after he learns of his family's incarceration and the retaliation efforts against other Mexicans. He surrenders to Jesús "El Teco" González and is turned over to a Texas Ranger near Laredo, Texas. Cortez is taken then to Karnes County where he is under the constant threat of lynching, and it is there that he is sentenced to "ninety-nine years and a day" for stealing a horse.[8] So says the legend. In reality, after a three-and-a-half-year legal battle, Gregorio Cortez was found guilty of Sheriff Glover's murder and sentenced to life in prison.[9] After twelve years of incarceration, Cortez was pardoned by Texas governor O. B. Colquitt and released in accordance with the recommendation of the Board of Pardons Advisors, which believed the applicant was innocent.[10]

Américo Paredes's rendition of the legend combined elements

from many narrators, who gathered around at night to tell stories and sing songs. Here, the anonymous voices of the Mexico-Tejano men speak for themselves, and the narration is told in a manner that captures the interest of the border folk and their hero.[11] Paredes anticipated other points of view in the study of culture because from this perspective Gregorio Cortez is not understood as a Mexican "bandit," but as the embodiment of the Mexico-Tejano's cultural values. He is a peaceful man goaded into violence, who defends his right with his pistol in his hand.

Paredes did more than simply collect and study the "survivals" of Spanish-Mexican folklore. He studied the development of this material in context as he had learned and performed these expressive models along the Lower Rio Grande region.[12] His approach to the ballad and legend of Gregorio Cortez emphasized the importance of performance, the context of performance, and the performers of folk poetry in order to question the representation of the Other as portrayed by North American authors. Songs, legends, and anecdotes of border conflict became the voice of the people, and Paredes recognized this development in the folklore of the Mexico-Tejano culture.

Culture conflict was the most important feature in Mexican American folklore, and the ballad of Gregorio Cortez epitomized this clash. The corrido thrived in situations of cultural conflict and began to supersede all other traditional ballad forms in the Lower Rio Grande region.

> Border balladry begins the century of conflict in diverse forms. As the *corrido* emerges, it assimilates the *romance* survivals that had come from Spain. Novelesque *romances* become definitely *corridos*, adapted to local conditions. One presumes the existence of some remnants of heroic *romances* in the echoes found in the language of the

> *corrido*. These, if they did exist, also were assimilated into the *corrido*. The *verso* almost completely disappears. The *décima* holds its own for some time, but toward the latter part of the period it is in neglect. Some *décimas* are remembered as *corridos* and their fragments are given the *corrido* form. The same thing that happens to the *décima* occurs to the newly arrived *danza*.[13]

If violent cultural confrontation had continued for a longer period, Américo Paredes believed that the border corrido would have assumed total hegemony over border balladry in general. He felt that the balladry along the Lower Rio Grande border was "working toward a single type: toward one form, the *corrido;* toward one theme, border conflict; toward one concept of the hero, the man fighting for his right with his pistol in hand."[14] Thus, the musical form of the corrido became a literature of resistance for Américo Paredes.

The Mexico-Tejano scholar exploded the myth of the Texas Rangers and the American West. Paredes's investigation of border balladry, from its origins in the Spanish romance to the rise of the Texas Mexican corrido, contradicted the legends of the Texas Rangers as daring, courageous, and the archetype of the Texas cowboy. At the beginning of Paredes's book, Hally Wood offers a translation of "El corrido de Gregorio Cortez":

> They let loose the bloodhound dogs;
> They followed him from afar.
> But trying to catch Cortez
> Was like following a star.
>
> All the rangers of the county
> Were flying, they rode so hard;

What they wanted was to get
The thousand-dollar reward.

And in the county of Kiansis
They cornered him after all;
Though they were more than three
hundred
He leaped out of their corral.

Then the Major Sheriff said,
As if he was going to cry,
"Cortez, hand over your weapons;
We want to take you alive."
Then said Gregorio Cortez,
And his voice was like a bell,
"You will never get my weapons
Till you put me in a cell."

Then said Gregorio Cortez,
With his pistol in his hand,
"Ah, so many mounted Rangers,
Just to take one Mexican!"

Although some verses of the corrido are highly exaggerated, many parts of the story appear to have been true. Cortez was chased by hundreds of men; he did kill another sheriff; and he did leap into the San Antonio River while astride his horse.[15] The ballad of Gregorio Cortez mocked the image of Texas Rangers as supposedly superior horsemen.

Paredes's section from his dissertation on the corrido's rise and fall, published separately the same year (1958), challenged Mexico's foremost ballad authority, Vicente Mendoza. He questioned the origins of the corrido as a ballad form as described in Mendoza's book *El corrido mexicano* (1954).[16] Américo Paredes suggested in his essay "The Mexican *Corrido*" that the corrido may have developed along the Lower Rio Grande border first and then spread to Greater Mexico.[17] It may not have been the other way around as Mendoza claimed. Paredes proposed that the border folk along the Lower Rio Grande region not only preserved the best qualities of the Spanish ballad tradition, but also took it to another level when they began to sing of themes related to culture conflict. Paredes suggested the plausibility of this occurrence in the development of the corrido.[18]

Américo Paredes understood the Mexico-Tejano culture as vital and dynamic, a concept that was rejected at the time. He demonstrated that although Mexican Americans had borrowed many aspects from Mexican culture, they also contributed to it with their own corridos. As the title of Paredes's work (*"With His Pistol in His Hand"*) suggests, the use of the pistol by Mexican American's preceded the use of that weapon by Mexicans in Mexico. Chicano folklore, moreover, was the first to make use of Anglicisms, like *cherife* (sheriff), rinches (Texas Rangers), and *jaunes* (bloodhounds). The Texas Rangers, the Walker Colt revolving six-shooter, the English language, the Spanish romance tradition, and Greater Mexican balladry in general influenced the corrido of border conflict.

Américo Paredes postulated in *"With His Pistol in His Hand"* that the essence of Chicano literature could be found in the common people's folklore. This idea suggested that earlier prevailing themes of "Spanishness" among certain authors who wrote in English was more of a response to the negative connotations of belonging to a conquered people. The attitudes expressed in the early English literature of Mexican Americans, according to Raymund A. Paredes, was "nostalgic and oddly detached from contemporary issues, as if the present reality were too painful to confront."[19] Writers like Nina Otero-Warren (*Old Spain in Our Southwest*, 1936), Cleofas M. Jaramillo (*Shadows of the Past [Sombras del Pasado]*, 1941) and Fabiola Cabeza de Baca (*We Fed Them Cactus*, 1954) dwell on the mystique of a romantic Spanish past and claim to be pure descendants of heroic Spanish conquistadores. Although there may be some validity to this claim, it is difficult to conceive from a people who resided for hundreds of years in a foreign land and among various ethnic groups.[20] Américo Paredes challenged the myth of the "Spanish Southwest," initiated in part by the works of Charles F. Lummis and Aurelio M. Espinosa.[21]

In terms of a Chicano literary style, Américo Paredes wrote in the Texas folklore tradition of authors like J. Frank Dobie, Alan and John Lomax, and Mody C. Boatright. His prose is "short on adjectives," "strong on active verbs," and accessible to a general audience.[22] The study of Greater Mexican folklore—plain and simple—influenced and informed his writing in *"With His Pistol in His Hand."* The book consists of scholarly research intertwined and juxtaposed with the oral history of the Mexico-Tejano folk where ballads, legends, and tales of the border folk make up his narrative. His approach to the written word reflects the name and poetic style of the corrido, taken from the verb *correr*, "which means to run or to flow . . . [telling] a story simply and swiftly without embellishments."[23] From a linguistic perspective, Américo Paredes transcribes as faithfully as possible Spanish words and phrases, such as *frente a frente* (front to front), *cherife mayor* (major sheriff), and *ver lo bonito* (a pretty thing to see), in order to remain loyal to Chicano expressive forms.

The narrative form of the *corrido* is discussed in part two, "El Corrido de Gregorio Cortez, a Ballad of Border Conflict." The arrangement of this ballad type consists of four-line octosyllabic stanzas, or quatrains, and the rhyme scheme of each quatrain is *abcb*. The independent quatrains are balanced into two equal parts of two lines each:

En/ el/ con/da/do/ de/ Car/nes (a)
mi/ren/ lo/ que ha/ su/ce/di/do, (b)
mu/rió/ el/ Che/ri/fe/ Ma/yor (c)
que/dan/do/ Ro/mán/ he/ri/do. (b)

Se/rían/ las/ dos/ de/ la/ tar/de (a)
cuan/do/ la/ gen/te/ lle/gó, (b)
u/nos/ a/ los/ ot/ros/ di/cen: (c)
—No/ sa/ben/ quién/ lo/ ma/tó. (b)

Se/ an/du/vie/ron/ in/for/man/do (a)
co/mo/ me/dia ho/ra/ des/pués, (b)
su/pie/ron/ que el/ mal/he/chor (c)
e/ra/ Gre/go/rio/ Cor/tez.[24] (b)

The folk song suggests the refining process of how to best relate a long story rapidly and swiftly. The formal opening of the corrido presents the scene and tone of the narrative and sets up the interrogation. It begins in medias res to capture the listener's attention. Paredes used a similar approach in his organization of chapter 2, "The Legend." The story begins after a traditional corrido performance, encouraging a dialogue to know more about the legend. The performer's role in the narration is that of a spectator, too, who calls for the attention of his audience. He is an anonymous actor and his creative act involves the re-creation of an event. At the time of the song, heightened with the accompaniment of music, the imperfect tense is used to create a fluid present in which singer, audience, and event are all present at once.[25] Américo Paredes employed many of these narrative techniques in *"With His Pistol in His Hand."*

If the independent quatrains of the corrido serve as imaginary, moving pictures (accompanied by music) for an oral community, the written stanzas serve as narrative "sketches" for readers of literature. Many years later Américo Paredes wanted to reorganize *"With His Pistol in His Hand"* into a series of sketches to better capture the cultural life of the border folk in all its multiplicity, but other responsibilities kept him from this project.[26] Analogous to the corrido, the "sketches" suggest a shifting of scenes, point of view, and time frame within the narration to offer many possible views of a particular event. The scenes swing back and forth and the point of view moves from protagonist, to adversaries, to common people alike. The time frame within the story can either be early, late, or in the middle of the story. The dialogue and drama within these compact scenes, moreover, allow the story to move swiftly and naturally. Since the border corrido is a composition in most cases (excluding broadside publications) of and for the folk, it possesses a local interest rather than a nationalistic agenda. The language is hybrid, and familiar places are observed within the narrative to serve as reflection of community interests.[27] These local interests generally make use of universal themes, like honor, respect, infidelity, and betrayal. The two components put together, content and form, translate into what can be understood as Américo Paredes's concept and function of writing.

"With His Pistol in His Hand" was practically "unknown and unread" for almost a decade after its publication, most likely a result of the poor enrollment of Chicanas and Chicanos in higher education.[28] Not until the mid-1960s did young Chicano activists at Berkeley and other California universities discover the book. They recognized its significance as an alternative to American

history, sociology, anthropology, and literature. Although Américo Paredes never actually claimed it, many felt that "*With His Pistol in His Hand*" was instrumental in the birth of the Chicano movement.[29]

What Some Scholars Have Said about "*With His Pistol in His Hand*"

Today, many critics have acknowledged the impact that "*With His Pistol in His Hand*" has had in the development of Chicano and U.S. Latino cultural studies. Some of the major figures in anthropology, ethnomusicology, film, folklore, history, literature, and contemporary music have stated frankly the decisive influence Américo Paredes's study has had on their literary, scholarly, and musical careers. Some of these individuals include Roger D. Abrahams, Richard Bauman, Gerard Béhague, Norma Cantú, Arturo Chamorro, Dan Dickey, Steven Feld, Richard R. Flores, Leticia M. Garza-Falcón, Alicia María González, William Gradante, Joe Graham, María Herrera-Sobek, Tish Hinojosa, Rolando Hinojosa-Smith, Pat Jasper, Deborah Kapchan, Luis Leal, Pauline López, John McDowell, James C. McNutt, Martha Menchaca, David Montejano, Olga Nájera-Ramírez, Mary Margaret Návar, Raymund A. Paredes, Manuel Peña, Lourdes Pérez, Severo Pérez, Tomás Rivera, Amalia Rodríguez-Mendoza, Ricardo Romo, Sonia Saldívar-Hull, John M. Schechter, Suzanne Seriff, Joel Sherzer, Nick Spitzer, Beverly J. Stoeltje, Kay Turner, and Anthony N. Zavaleta. The Mexico-Tejano intellectual was quite influential among the scholars he directly mentored and with others at other campuses, particularly, but not limited to Chicanos and Chicanas.

Those scholars would agree that Américo Paredes was a pioneer in Mexican American cultural studies, and I discuss briefly some scholarly interpretations of "*With His Pistol in His Hand*," such as those by Ramón and José David Saldívar, José E. Limón, Renato Rosaldo, and Héctor Calderón. Each of these critics argues from a different perspective how the book teaches the important relationship between art and history, how it deconstructs Texas history, how the text prefigures the "crisis" in cultural anthropology, and how Paredes's stance as a writer speaks to the heart of much of Chicano literature. At least two of these authors do not approve of Paredes's idyllic picture of the Mexico-Tejano culture before U.S. expansionism, suggesting that Américo Paredes romanticized the past. Yet all these scholars acknowledge "El corrido de Gregorio Cortez" as folklore as performance, and my research builds on this argument with the discussion of another item of performance in *"With His Pistol in His Hand."* Gregorio's brother Román is an interpreter of folklore, too, although of a different and less obvious type than the traditional performance of the corrido. He is a folk poet of jests, and his creative performance as a dumb Mexican at the time of the horse trade is central to the legend of Gregorio Cortez.

Ramón Saldívar was one of the first scholars to offer a comprehensive study of *"With His Pistol in His Hand"* in his book *Chicano Narrative: The Dialectics of Difference* (1990). The Stanford professor's approach mirrors Paredes's book in that he uses history, folklore, anthropology, and literary criticism to demonstrate the birth of Chicano studies. Saldívar's analysis consists of the history behind the Spanish romance's thematic and lyrical transformation into the corrido of border conflict; the narrative strategies used to communicate the legend; the importance of folk song performances as a socially symbolic act; and the influence Paredes's book had on other Chicano writers like Tomás Rivera and Rolando Hinojosa-Smith. Saldívar states that *"With His Pistol in His Hand"* serves as a model of instruction for future Chicano writers because it teaches the interrelationship between art and history.[30] He closes his book by claiming that cultural resistance is a characteristic in the aesthetic nature of Chicano expression.

José David Saldívar (Ramón's younger brother) offers another perspective of "*With His Pistol in His Hand*" in his article "Chicano Border Narratives as Cultural Critique" (1991).[31] He analyzes the works of Américo Paredes, Tomás Rivera, and Rolando Hinojosa to illustrate a unique Mexico-Tejano response to the political and ideological rhetoric of south Texas.[32] José David Saldívar stresses Américo Paredes's creativity, intelligence, and courage to challenge the authority of Walter Prescott Webb. He also cites how Webb's best-selling account of the Texas Rangers was so popular that Paramount Pictures purchased the film rights to the book for eleven thousand dollars.[33] Neither the film, *The Texas Rangers*, nor its sequel, *The Texas Rangers Ride Again*, addresses the racial strife between the Texas Rangers and Mexico-Tejanos. José David Saldívar concludes that "*With His Pistol in His Hand*" is the first Chicano text to overturn the established discourses in Texas.

José E. Limón was a student of Américo Paredes, and he has written extensively on "*With His Pistol in His Hand*." His contributions include *Mexican Ballads, Chicano Poems: History and Influence in Mexican-American Social Poetry* (1992), *Dancing with the Devil: Society and Cultural Poetics in Mexican-American South Texas* (1994), and "The Return of the Mexican Ballad: Américo Paredes and His Anthropological Text as Persuasive Political Performances" (1993).

In his two books, Limón situates Paredes's study within its historical context to emphasize the impact Américo Paredes's scholarship had within the university's literary and folkloric traditions. Once Limón positions "*With His Pistol in His Hand*" at the center of both of his own studies, the author uses Paredes's work as a point of departure to examine developments in Chicana and Chicano poetry and folklore material. Specifically, in *Mexican Ballads, Chi-*

cano Poems José E. Limón notes how Américo Paredes's method of writing foreshadows the narrative strategies suggested for anthropology's "experimental moment,"[34] and in *Dancing with the Devil*, he criticizes Américo Paredes's romantic and idealized view of the border folk that excluded "an emerging Mexican-American middle class."[35]

The idea that Américo Paredes's life and work prefigure the trends in cultural anthropology is made by José E. Limón in his important essay "Return of the Mexican Ballad." Limón notes how Paredes used humor, irony, and inversion to critique Texas history with regard to Mexican stereotypes, and how *"With His Pistol in His Hand"* was exemplary in the postmodern concepts that deal with the representation of culture. The idea that Américo Parédes was ahead of his time and that he anticipated some of the postmodern trends in cultural anthropology is discussed in the next chapter.

Renato Rosaldo, a New York University anthropologist, explains Américo Paredes's use of a unified subject (Gregorio Cortez) to challenge negative stereotypes of Mexicans, and discusses how he uses a creative writing style to critique the history of Texas. In his book *Culture and Truth: The Remaking of Social Analysis* (1993), Rosaldo states that *"With His Pistol in His Hand"* is without precedent—its timing parallels Fidel Castro and Ernesto "Che" Guevara's fight against U.S. imperialism in Cuba; it antedates the Chicano political movement by about a decade; and it foreshadows the development of Chicano studies.[36] Rosaldo explains, moreover, Américo's use of humor as a viable source of Mexican American identity and resistance and questions Paredes's re-creation of a tranquil mestizo culture along the Lower Rio Grande border. Like José E. Limón, Renato Rosaldo recognizes the importance of Américo Paredes's work in postmodern anthropology by arguing that Américo Paredes was among the first to recognize the play between cultural groups and power.[37]

For Héctor Calderón the U.S.-Mexican border is reinvented from an Anglo-American concept to a Chicano perspective in "*With His Pistol in His Hand.*" In his essay "Reinventing the Border" (1995) the UCLA scholar suggests that it was Américo Paredes's talents as a writer that made the Chicana/o genre possible.[38] He calls attention to Américo's disappearing act as a writer in chapter 2, "The Legend," to transcribe and translate a group's storytelling performance. And according to Calderón, this narrative stance as an ethnographer taken by Paredes represents the "inner form of much Chicano fiction."[39]

Héctor Calderón's theory differs from Ramón Saldívar's perspective with regard to the essence of Chicana/o literature. Both agree that cultural conflict plays an important role in shaping the consciousness and identity of Mexican Americans. Yet, for Ramón Saldívar the study of the border corrido tradition "may be" the invention of a Chicano narrative community, since it is the "imaginative seeding ground" for the development of Chicano fiction. Paredes's study combines the elements of art and history and teaches the important interrelationship between the two.[40] While other books treated the Mexican American experience before the publication of "*With His Pistol in His Hand,*" there is, according to Saldívar, something different about Paredes's book. It stands alone in historical, aesthetic, and theoretical terms in the development of Chicano literature as the book responds to the imposition of North American culture.[41]

Héctor Calderón, on the other hand, focuses on Paredes's creative energies as a talented writer. He believes it was Américo Paredes's ability to capture the subtle idiosyncrasies of Mexican American culture that made the Chicano narrative possible. The different perspectives taken by these two critics appear to be one of content and form, and how one may interpret "Chicana/o" and "literature."[42] Saldívar's view of "*With His Pistol in His Hand*" represents a type of Chicano literature when cultural conflict is taken to be the most important aspect, while for Calderón it is one of style. He believes that Paredes's narrative techniques—such as dramatic dialogue, journalistic broadside, and scenic representation—are the creative aspects used in much of contemporary Mexican American fiction.

José Limón and Renato Rosaldo also raise an important issue with regard to class along the Lower Rio Grande region. According to Américo Paredes there was no distinction in terms of class, and the ranching way of life would have continued to develop had it not been for U.S. expansionism.[43] But a closer examination of the Mexico-Tejano culture along the Lower Rio Grande border points to centuries of conflict with Indians from the interior of Mexico and later with the Apache and Comanche from the north. The establishment of a feudal-like economy, moreover, was in sharp contrast to North American capitalism. The method of colonial settlement introduced by the Spanish Crown to assimilate the native population into a European culture in many ways stagnated the societies. To believe this patriarchal society based on feudal land tenure and peonage would flourish and develop is problematic.[44] A hierarchical society was present and significant within the Lower Rio Grande communities, although Américo Paredes proposes otherwise in his text: "The simple pastoral life led by most Border people fostered a natural equality among men. Much has been written about the democratizing influence of a horse culture. More important, was the fact that on the Border the landowner lived and worked upon his land. There was almost no gap between the owner and his cowhand, who often was related to him anyway. The simplicity of the life led by both employer and employee also helped make them feel that they were not different kinds of men, even if one was richer than the other."[45] Paredes did suggest that the "peon . . . could and did rise in the social scale," though the presentation of an idyllic ranching culture is problematic.[46] The feudal-like economy established along the Lower Rio Grande region had its imperfections as does any other society, and the socioeconomic mobility among the poor mestizo class was practically nonexistent according to some people. In many cases, the peones blindly obeyed the orders of their masters.[47] The Texas folklorist Jovita González even suggested that the peones benefited the most from the change in economy because it represented better opportunities for them.[48]

The fact that the North Americans encountered a society on the border that was divided along class lines had its lasting effects. The majority of the new Anglo immigrants were neither rich nor poor, but what they found among the Mexico-Tejanos was far from an egalitarian society. The American ethnologist and folklorist John G. Bourke observed in 1894 the presence of an elite class in south Texas: "Stress cannot be too pointedly laid upon the existence within this Dark Belt of thriving, intelligent communities, such as Brownsville, Matamoros, Corpus Christi, Laredo, San Diego, and others, in which are to be found people of as much refinement and good breeding as anywhere else in the world, but exerting about as much influence upon the *indigenes* around them as did the Saxon or Danish invaders upon the Celts in Ireland."[49] Carey McWilliams also discussed the feudal-like system as an important difference between the two cultures in his book *North from Mexico* (1949): "The absence of local self-government and the presence of a population that was seven-eighths illiterate in 1850, predisposed the Anglo-Americans to form an extremely negative opinion of the Mexican lower classes who [constituted] nine-tenths of the population. If a larger middle-class element had existed, the adjustment between the two cultures might have been facilitated and the amount of intermarriage might have been greater. The subordinate status of the *pobres* in relation to the *ricos*, and their property, served to set them apart in a category that, in Anglo-American eyes, was roughly comparable to that of the Indians."[50] Like most arguments of this nature, chances are that the relationship between rich and poor was somewhere in the middle. Both types of classes existed along the Lower Rio Grande border, and there must have been some sort of socioeconomic mobility in some instances. But unquestionably North Americans frowned upon miscegenation. Many Anglo-Americans, as a result, concerned themselves primarily with the negative aspects of the Mexican character, and many of them perpetuated these feelings in thought and action throughout the American Southwest as a way to justify U.S. expansionism.

Additionally, Craig Stinson brings into focus this type of argumentation that deals with the internal conflicts of the Lower Rio Grande border culture and its patriarchal traditions. "What Paredes did in the late 1950s was revolutionary and has helped facilitate the framework many of the current scholars enjoy" today.[51] The emphasis and approach toward culture and minority groups has changed considerably in academic research, and scholars like Américo Paredes contributed significantly to this shift.

Another Example of Folklore as Performance

Which brings us to Américo Paredes's idea of folklore as performance as an important theme in *"With His Pistol in His Hand."* The folk poets along the Lower Rio Grande border were very much aware of the racial attitudes of the time. They expressed this in the performance of songs, legends, jests, and anecdotes, with both overt and subtle manifestations that conveyed the tension and hostility between Anglos and Mexico-Tejanos. The first (which many have discussed) involves a traditional performance of a corrido where the folk "sing with deadly-serious faces, throwing out the words of the song like a challenge, tearing savagely with their stiff, callused fingers at the strings of the guitars."[52] There is a roughness to the element of performance, it is raw and unyielding. But equally important is the sly, creative interpretation of folklore, the type that rarely make headlines. To act dumb and play the part of the lazy Mexican became a sort of weapon for the border folk, and Américo Paredes was sensitive to this sort of behavior. His book aligns itself with James C. Scott's anthropological study *Weapons of the Weak: Everyday Forms of Peasant Resistance* (1985) in that dissimulation, or "playing the part," becomes a type of behavior for a culture that has been rendered politically and economically powerless. Scott recognizes that oppressed groups always adopt a protective mask in their relationship with those in power and that this disguise is apparent in both conformity and resistance to the status quo. Thus, "foot dragging, dissimulation, desertion, false compliance, pilfering, feigned ignorance, slander, arson, [and] sabotage" can all be considered as weapons of the poor.[53]

Román Cortez may be included in the list of jokesters. In another of Paredes's literary renditions—one that also can be considered as ethnography—Gregorio's brother plays the role of the dumb Mexican to separate the Anglo-American from his horse. Román knows that if he acts as anything but a stupid Mexican, the gringo will get suspicious, so he plays the part and the Anglo-Texan thinks it will be easy to take advantage of him.

> Román owned two horses, two beautiful sorrels that were just alike, the same color, the same markings, and the same size. You could not have told them apart, except that one of them was lame. There was an American who owned a little sorrel mare. This man was dying to get Román's sorrel—the good one—and every time they met he would offer to swap the mare for the horse. But Román did not

> think much of the mare. He did not like it when the American kept trying to make him trade.
>
> "I wonder what this Gringo thinks," Román said to himself. "He takes me for a fool. But I'm going to make him such a trade that he will remember me forever."
>
> And Román laughed a big-mouthed laugh. He thought it would be a fine joke, besides a good trade. . . . So, Román saddled the lame sorrel, led him a little way along the road, and stopped under a big mesquite that bordered on the fence. He fixed it so the spavined side was against the mesquite. Román waited a little while. . . . When the American came around the bend, there was Román on his sorrel horse. The American stopped his buggy beside Román and looked at the horse with much admiration. . . .
>
> "Changed your mind?" the American said.
>
> Román stopped chewing on a mesquite and said, "Changed my mind about what?"
>
> "About trading that horse for my mare."
>
> "You're dead set on trading your mare for this horse of mine?" Román said.
>
> "You know I am," the American said. "Are you ready to come round?"
>
> "I'm in a trading mood," said Román. "With just a little arguing you might convince me to trade this horse for that worthless mare of yours. But I don't know; you might go back on the deal later on."[54]

Román's cleverness allows him to pull off the horse trade.[55] The Anglo-Texan was too quick to accept as genuine the Mexican persona that corresponded with his own prejudices. And his biases are expressed before and after the horse trade with comments like:

"I never go back on my word. . . . What do you think I am, a Mexican?" And, "Now isn't that just like a Mexican. He takes his time."[56] Román's performance as a dumb Mexican fools the Anglo-Texan completely.

When Sheriff Morris and Ben Choate visit the Cortez residence to investigate a possible horse theft, Román continues to poke fun at the Anglo-Texans. Their inability to speak Spanish well and their lack of knowledge of the vaquero culture produce a sense of satisfaction in Gregorio's brother. His open-faced laughter humiliates and exacerbates Morris's ineptitude for not recognizing the difference between a horse and mare. Román's behavior infuriates Sheriff Morris so much that the Anglo-Texan shoots the Mexican through the mouth.

Américo Paredes made a point about the relationship between these two dominant groups in Texas and demonstrated with this exchange how poorly outsiders understood the Mexican people. Américo Paredes presented a distinct view of a population that few scholars and writers understood. The Mexico-Tejano scholar had mastered the anthropological techniques, methodologies, and theories of his time and he had observed a weakness. Outsiders (Anglo-Americans, anthropologists, ethnologists) never presumed that minority groups had the nerve to trick them. Mexican American performances often served as a protective disguise in their public and private dealings with the North Americans, and most writers were simply not well equipped to uncover the silent and anonymous forms of cultural resistance that in many ways characterized the border folk. Américo Paredes believed that in order for scholars to arrive at a more precise interpretation of folklore data and to fully understand its significance, the material needed to be studied and appreciated within its social context and with a particular awareness of the folk artist. The performance-oriented approach to folklore allowed him to better understand the psyche and reality of the Mexico-Tejano in relationship to the Anglo-American and his society. His concept of performance, coupled with his literary talents as a writer, in time would be articulated into a theoretical position for the study of culture.

The Motion Picture *The Ballad of Gregorio Cortez*

"With His Pistol in His Hand" eventually achieved considerable recognition, and Américo Paredes built up a fine reputation as an exceptional scholar. By 1982 the book had been turned into a film titled *The Ballad of Gregorio Cortez* (1984). The low-budget motion picture starred Edward James Olmos as Gregorio Cortez, Pepe Serna as Romaldo (Román), Timothy Scott as Sheriff Morris, and Tom Bower as Boone Choate. Other actors included James Gammon as Sheriff Frank Fly, Barry Corbin as the defense lawyer R. B. Abernathy, and Rosana DeSoto as Carlota Muñoz, the interpreter in the jail scene. The 106-minute color film was produced by Moctesuma Esparza and Michael Hausman and directed by Robert M. Young. It was funded by the National Endowment for the Humanities and the Corporation for Public Broadcasting. Overall, the movie adapts certain sections of the book well, with short scenes one after the other; the cinematography is excellent—especially during the Cortez chase; while the observation and interrogation of the *San Antonio Express* reporter, Bill Blakely (Bruce McGill), helps the viewer understand the reason for the chase. And as Rosa Linda Fregoso points out, Blakely's "fact-gathering" process for all to witness "provides a 'factual' basis for the film."[57]

In addition, the Anglo-Texan's English dialect and the Mexican's colloquial Spanish in the video illustrate one of the principal barriers that existed between the two groups. The two groups' inability to communicate is later made apparent when Gregorio Cortez meets a lonely Anglo cowboy in the late evening during his flight toward freedom. The man offers him food and friendship, although neither can understand each other. As the film critic Victor A. Sorell states, "the encounter is a human moment when two *vaqueros* of different cultures are shown to be more alike than different."[58] That common experience will be short-lived, however, and the incident is in stark contrast to Cortez's capture and incarceration. A hate-filled, prejudiced mob outside the prison wants the Mexican "bandit" turned over to them. These two scenes bring into focus some of the contradictions and misunderstandings in Texas society between the Anglo and Mexican American people.

But the film does have its weaknesses, especially for many Chicana and Chicano critics.[59] As Tatcho Mindiola makes clear, the movie is mostly about "the Anglo community and its reaction to the killing of an Anglo sheriff by Gregorio Cortez."[60] The horse trade between Román and the Anglo-Texan, an important theme in the legend of Gregorio Cortez, is not included in the movie. The exchange stresses Américo Paredes's concept of folklore as performance and without this scene a Mexican perspective toward the Anglo-Texan is not present. For example, what are some of the attitudes the Mexican has toward the Anglo in Texas in the movie? Why did border corridos become important for the people? Was it not important for Américo Paredes to offer another point of view in his book? Without this perspective, as Tatcho Mindiola explains, the viewer cannot fully capture or experience what life was like at that time for a Mexican in Texas because the focus is not on them or their views. "The audience does not come away from the film with a sense of how Mexicans in South Texas lived in 1901 and more importantly, how they felt and reacted to the events involving Gregorio Cortez. A sense of injustice against Mexicans is conveyed but again it comes from Anglos and the manner in which they acted and talked about Mexicans. How the Mexican community feels about the injustices they encounter is never present."[61] The Anglo-Texan's position toward the Mexican in the film is clear, but the attitudes of the Mexican people are not. Thus, the film tells a story about the Anglo community and the Texas Rangers rather than recounting the lives of the Mexican people as personified in Gregorio Cortez.

The lack of a Mexican perspective is further exemplified with the choice of music in the film. Viewers who expect to hear the tunes that expressed the heart and soul of the border communities with folk poets that "sing with deadly-serious faces, throwing out the words of a song like a challenge, tearing savagely with their stiff, callused fingers at the strings of the guitars" will be disappointed.[62] During the Cortez chase, the sounds of synthesizers abound, not traditional folk music. The use of technomusic in the train scene chase suggests how industrialization facilitated the western expansion of the United States as it minimized the importance of the Mexican vaquero culture.[63] Once again, North American dominance is identified and reinforced in image, thought, and sound, while the Mexican way of life remains mute.

Perhaps the most controversial theme of the film is the portrayal of Gregorio Cortez, a subject that bothered Américo Paredes a great deal.[64] At one point Gregorio Cortez is pictured as a savage, long-haired and dirty, unable to speak, and eating his food like a caveman. In another scene he is in a cantina, a beaten man who is barely able to eat his food, and still later he is in a jail cell, lying almost in a fetal position, emotionally and physically exhausted after the ordeal. Américo Paredes felt that these particular scenes robbed Gregorio Cortez of his dignity and courage.[65] The young actor himself, Edward James Olmos, responded to such criticism by stating that it was his intent "to portray Gregorio Cortez as a 'human being' and not as a 'macho.'"[66] But this is to confuse culture with politics because Cortez's characterization lacks the heroic qualities expressed in the corridos of border conflict. Instead, he is depicted as a victim of society, an object of study, and a spectacle for all to see. What mattered in the movie is what the Anglo community, not the Mexican community, thought about Cortez. Once more the silent minority is resurrected and reinforced for the American public, this time in film. Ironically, these were precisely the types of Mexican representations that Américo Paredes challenged and fought so hard against throughout much of his career.

Chapter 4

Toward New Perspectives in Folklore and Cultural Anthropology

The "I'm just a poor, dumb Mexican peon" persona is a favorite with the border Mexican jokester, who can use it for plain fun among his own group . . . or work it on outsiders with a barbed intent.

"On Ethnographic Work among Minority Groups: A Folklorist's Perspective"—Américo Paredes

A principal claim of this book is that Américo Paredes articulated an idea of performance that anticipated the postmodern movement in cultural anthropology—a movement that inspires the protection of primitive and local cultures from First World attempts to reorganize them. His take on cultural performance foreshadows a trend in contemporary anthropology that seeks a method of writing that is more culturally "sensitive to its broader political, historical, and philosophical implications."[1] Américo Paredes's shift from the study of "survival" items in folklore research to an examination of the creative responses of individuals under observation offered another point of view, a theme seldom acknowledged in the history of American anthropology. The spin allowed for Mexican Americans to share their attitudes of what they thought North Americans thought about them, since for so long Anglo-Americans had expressed their opinions in print about the Mexican people. Paredes's literary talents as a writer and cross-disciplinary perspectives in the study of culture are central to anthropology's "experimental moment" and its ethnographic "predicament" as expressed by Marcus and Fischer (1986) and Clifford (1988). The Mexico-Tejano folklorist has been underestimated as a cultural anthropologist, and yet his work is exemplary with regard to recent developments in the social sciences. But before I present some of Américo Paredes's contributions to this discipline, it is necessary to say a few words about American anthropology, its relationship to folklore, and its move from a "classic" period into a postmodern moment.

The Evolution of American Anthropology in the United States

Anthropology, the science of humankind, includes four areas—archeology, anthropological linguistics, biological anthropology and cultural anthropology—and a basic concept in the field is the study of "culture." Traditional anthropologists generally agree that culture is "that complex whole which includes knowledge, belief, art, law, morals, custom, and any other capabilities and habits acquired by man as a member of society."[2] Of these four branches of anthropology, cultural anthropology is considered to be the largest and the one most similar to folklore in its study of oral tradition. The two disciplines are even more alike when the folklorist records, examines, and interprets the function of folklore items rather than concentrates on the origin or diffusion of these expressive forms.[3] In other words, for these anthropologists it's not so much about what folklore is, where it came from, or how it's passed on—a concern that has not been abandoned—it's more about what folklore does for the people. What is special about folklore is the when, where, and why people perform its items, its context and situation, and Américo Paredes's work is important in this regard.

When an anthropologist travels to study and record the way of life of another people, the fieldworker describes on paper, tape, or film what he or she actually sees and understands about another culture. Bronislaw Malinowski (1884–1942), a British anthropologist, set the standard for this method of research known as ethnography, encouraging close contact with the informants over a long period of time.[4] The field report can include information about farming practices, ownership of the land, kinship, dress, music, dance, legal systems, and religion. And one objective of the anthropologist's "testimony" is to learn about the people and their culture in order to make available other ways of living for humankind. Since ethnography requires observing, writing, and understanding from an "outside" position, this type of work must also involve some type of theory, because an anthropologist cannot write about another people without ultimately making choices about what he or she thinks about the Other.[5] Thus, one of the most important goals of anthropology is to appreciate cultural difference and to recognize that diversity is advantageous for humankind, an opinion that was rarely considered in the United States until the beginning of the twentieth century.[6] This knowledge about another community is incomplete, however, if such elements as songs, legends, and jests are not considered a major part of the people's everyday lives. And from this position, language proficiency is fundamental in understanding the group and their expressive behavior. Folklore is one of the "universals" that all societies share and have in common, regardless of language, time, and location, because the people's lore is their history or collective memory.

The founder of American anthropology is Franz Boas (1858–

1942), a Jewish emigrant from Germany who began his career in the United States in 1888. Boas attacked the general attitude that cultures evolved in stages from savagery through barbarism to civilization and that the study of "primitive" cultures could furnish information about the ancestors of modern man. Cultural evolutionism, the dominant paradigm in the social sciences since the late nineteenth century, was a racist theory that the Columbia professor refused to accept. It was a hypothesis that had not been proven by comparative studies as advocated by evolutionists. Boas argued his point in his 1896 essay titled "The Limitations of the Comparative Method in Anthropology." "It must, therefore, be clearly understood," Boas maintained, "that anthropological research which compares similar cultural phenomena from various parts of the world, in order to discover the uniform history of their development, makes the assumption that the same ethnological phenomenon has everywhere developed in the same manner. Here lies the flaw in the argument of the new method, for no such proof can be given. Even the most cursory review shows that the same phenomenon may develop in a multitude of ways."[7] In Boas's view, to treat cultural items like totems, geometrical designs, and the use of masks as universals was incorrect because these objects may have each developed from different sources. Thus, an evaluation could not be made until there was proof that the material under study was right for comparison.[8]

Instead, the Columbia anthropologist suggested another course in anthropological research. "The object of investigation is to find the *processes* by which certain stages of culture have developed. The customs and beliefs themselves are not the ultimate objects of research. We desire to learn the reasons why such customs and beliefs exist—in other words, we wish to discover the history of their development."[9] In order to truly understand a culture, it was essential to set aside predisposed standards or expectations since for Boas culture was best understood on it own terms, within its own context, and within its own history. It was wrong to consider one's inner prejudices in an attempt to understand a new culture. Rather than comparing it to one's own way of life, contact and experiences with other people and cultures should generate new ways of thinking and provide an opportunity to understand one's own cultural background from a whole new perspective. And contrary to the general attitude of the time, Boas rejected the idea that there were biologically "pure" races as a consequence of historical "intermingling," and instead believed that the "mixture" of races had no harmful consequences on humankind.[10] Unlike the "armchair" theorists of the late nineteenth century who had little or no contact with primitive peoples, Franz Boas insisted that ethnographers learn the native language, conduct fieldwork, and study the history of a culture to gain an insider's point of view. His idea of "being there" hinted at the relationship between the individual and society and supported his belief of cultural diversity over evolutionism.[11] And even though Boas did make comparisons in the area of folklore, the founder of American anthropology was convinced that cultures were "relative" and that an individual was to be judged by his or her moral faculties.

In the 1920s and 1930s the students of Franz Boas took his ideas a step further and challenged the certainties of Western civilization. These anthropologists included Margaret Mead, Edward Sapir, Elsie Clews Parsons, and Ruth Benedict, and they championed their mentor's project of relativism to criticize the conditions in American society.[12] As early cultural critics they expressed sympathy for their subjects and dissatisfaction with their own privileged lives.[13] Ruth Benedict in particular became "a transitional figure who moved both anthropology and folklore away from the narrow confines of culture-trait diffusion studies toward theories of performance as expressive aspects of cultural configuration."[14] She argued that certain aspects of culture needed to be understood in social context for accurate interpretations, and her work influenced Américo Paredes. Benedict was a professor of folklore in the anthropology department at Columbia University for twenty-three years (1925–48) and editor of the *Journal of American Folklore* for fourteen of those years (1925–39).[15]

The period between 1945 and 1970 was a difficult time for the United States. World War II, the Korean War, the civil rights movement, and the Vietnam War all played a role in the trajectory of American anthropology, particularly with regard to the writing of it. The era of revolution was marked by the fact that more than sixty countries around the world "attained their political independence from colonial rule."[16] Realistically, the classic period of the anthropologist who traveled to far-off lands to study and record the life of an isolated community was not as viable as in the past. The world was much more interconnected than previously imagined and colonial subjects were much more conscious of the practices of domination. The relationship between the observer and the observed had changed and could no longer be taken for granted by contemporary anthropologists. In the United States, for example, minority groups had played vital roles in World War II and the Korean War, and they expected equal treatment and full participation in American society. Many attended universities and colleges under the GI Bill and began to have an impact on American institutions in the late 1950s and early 1960s. These groups celebrated their cultural heritages, challenged the status quo, and questioned North American interpretations of their people. Times had changed, and certain minority groups assimilated knowledge expressed about them as part of their identities to undermine the authority of ethnographic discourse.

Américo Paredes Explores the Reality of Mexican Americans from a Variety of Perspectives in the 1960s and 1970s

During the rise of the Chicano movement, Américo Paredes's "*With His Pistol in His Hand*" was discovered, and it provided young activists with a convincing literary account of Mexican American resistance against U.S. hegemony. At this time Américo Paredes continued to articulate his idea of folklore as performance at the University at Texas at Austin, and he teamed up with Roger D. Abrahams and Richard Bauman to promote a performance-oriented approach in folklore research. Many of his essays from this period exemplify his experimentation with the notion of performance, a theory that became a central theme of reference in his writings and one that combined his literary, musical, and anthropological interests to reinterpret previous stereotypes of Mexican Americans

Américo Paredes linked poetic form with performance in one of his first essays titled "Some Aspects in Folk Poetry" (1964). He examined folk poetry on its own terms to demonstrate its value and uniqueness in spite of its simplicity in comparison to sophisticated literature. According to the Mexico-Tejano performer, written poetry was much more complex and multifaceted because it had removed itself farther and farther from the spoken word. A tendency of sophisticated literature, therefore, was toward individual modes of expression that attempted to be striking and original. Unlike folk poetry, the interaction between poet and public was no longer necessary in view of the fact that the context was different. The process now involved the "act of private communication between poet and reader."[17]

Folk poetry, on the other hand, made use of a highly conventional language and a simple balanced, binary structure. This poetry did not need to be complicated in terminology and style; it retained a sense of immediacy because it was performed. For Paredes, this element was essential to folk poetry because the performer made all the difference with regard to his material. "The performer . . . is an actor, a personality. In the comic song he may play the clown. In the folksong of high seriousness he will be serious; he will take a detached attitude toward himself as performer. But he is far from detached in respect to his subject. On the contrary, it is a supreme involvement that gives him the intense style that is often called impersonality."[18] Like the writer of sophisticated literature the folk poet was an artist, and Paredes underscored the importance of performance, the context of performance, and the performer of folk poetry to highlight some of the conditions necessary to understand folk poetry. At family gatherings or intimate settings, folk songs were given temporary life through performances, and it was the performer's interpretation of the material that gave it a power and passion often lost in written expression. In the end, Paredes wanted to make a point with his essay "Some Aspects of Folk Poetry." He wanted to do away with any preconceived notions of value or taste between sophisticated literature and folk poetry, and he demonstrated how the context of each was different in his attempt to place both on the same level of significance.

Musically, folklore as performance is evident in many of Paredes's works during this period, including essays such as "The *Décima Cantada* on the Texas-Mexican Border" (1966), "The *Décima* on the Texas-Mexican Border" (1966), "El concepto de la 'médula emotiva' aplicado al corrido mexicano 'Benjamín Argumedo'" (1972), "José Mosqueda and the Folklorization of Actual Events" (1973), "'El romance de la Isla de Jauja' en el suroeste de Estados Unidos" (1978), and his book *A Texas-Mexican Cancionero* (1976). All these writings emphasize the importance of songs to understand culture, and the music is examined from various perspectives. "The *Décima Cantada* on the Texas-Mexican Border," co-written with George Foss, is a good example of how this type of folk song was sung along the Lower Rio Grande region. As Paredes and Foss point out, although this song with its ten-line stanza and intricate rhyme scheme may appear to be rigid in poetic form, the performance involved is not as monotonous or mechanical as one might expect it to be. "The *décima cantada* achieves an effect of freedom and variety not found in many other, more loosely structured songs."[19] The décima can be performed with or without musical accompaniment, and it is the *parlando-rubato* style (speaking and chanting out of time, musically) that is usually preferred.

As an anthropologist, Américo Paredes reveals the different layers of folk tradition and the function of particular jokes through his performance-oriented approach in his essay "Folk Medicine and the Intercultural Jest" (1968). The material involves *curanderos* (Mexican folk doctors), *casos* (belief tales about curandero practices), and *tallas* (joking sessions that make fun of these medicinal remedies), and to properly interpret the ethnographic data, the anthropologist should know something about *curanderismo*, the identity of the performer, and the dynamics of the context in which the stories are told. In this case, the jests are being performed by professional Mexican American males that live in an in-between existence, socially, culturally, and economically. This fragmentation or conflict is revealed in the material. "It is this double nature of our texts that makes them especially interesting. In the satirizing of folk medicine and curandero belief tales they express a mocking rejection of Mexican folk culture; in their expression of resentment toward American culture they show a strong sense of identification with the Mexican folk."[20] The jests revealed mixed emotions, ranging from exasperation to a deep sense of affection toward the Mexican immigrant intermingled with a resentment and masked outrage toward the United States.

In spite of their acculturation, these Mexico-Tejanos still considered themselves as *mexicanos* because the North American culture had never really accepted them as Americans. Their attitude caused them to identify with the struggle of Mexican peasant groups, since they were in a position to foresee many of their troubles in a different society.

Toward New Perspectives in Folklore (1972), edited by Américo Paredes and Richard Bauman, proved to be pivotal in the history of folklore research in the United States. The book was a reprint of a special issue of the *Journal of American Folklore* from the previous year (1971), was revisited twenty years later in a special issue by *Western Folklore* (1993), and was reprinted by Trickster Press in 2000. *Toward New Perspectives in Folklore* illustrates the shift in focus from the traditional items of analysis to the process of folklore and the politics of culture. As in the study of folklore, the notion of performance was becoming a principal concept in linguistic anthropology and a reason to merge similar ways of thinking between the two disciplines.[21] The thirteen contributors—Roger D. Abrahams, Richard Bauman, Dan Ben-Amos, Alan Dundes, Kenneth S. Goldstein, Gary Gossen, Dell Hymes, Heda Jason, Elli Kongas Maranda, Robert J. Smith, Brian Stross, Brian Sutton-Smith, and Dennis Tedlock—use concepts from anthropology, folklore, literary criticism, linguistics, psychology, and sociology in their study of folklore. All these scholars recognized the role of performance as an "organizing principle" and as a point of departure to examine more carefully the "artistic act, expressive form, and esthetic response," in its natural context.[22] Folklore was now best understood as, in the words of Dan Ben-Amos, "artistic communication in small groups."[23] The book clearly demonstrated the trend in folklore studies toward a performance-oriented method at UT, Austin, and a break from the traditional literary approach of the Texas

Folklore Society. The performance model shaped the theory of folklore research for years to come and it foreshadowed a literary turn in contemporary anthropology, an "experimental moment" that called for a change in the practice of cultural representation. Whether one accepts the new language to understand cultural anthropology's shift from a classical period into a postmodern age is a matter of choice, but what cannot be ignored is that the writing of culture became much more problematic and controversial than it once was.

A Few Words about the Postmodern Movement in Cultural Anthropology

According to advocates of postmodernism, the philosophy celebrates difference because diversity is understood as good for humankind.[24] "And the more, the better," they would say. Any attempt to silence an alternative point of view is seen as unjust and undemocratic given that there are many ways to look at the world and no one vision or "totalizing discourse" is correct. For these enthusiasts any doctrine that is all-encompassing or that claims to be a grand theory about science, theology, and politics is defined as "modernist" and looked upon with suspicion and antagonism. Postmodernists detest any sort of hierarchy that is based on illegitimate power and used as a tool to oppress and silence people. The movement and its followers believe that a space for difference in all aspects of civilization is vital to humankind, and for this reason they are in favor of smaller, local discourses. Specifically in the field of cultural anthropology, postmodernists "oppose the presumption of ethnological authority on the part of the anthropologist."[25] They favor an ethnography that reflects the unequal relationship between the observers and observed, a writing that is multifaceted or from various point of views, and one that exhibits the potentialities of humankind and not its limitations. Once again, Paredes's work is significant in this area.

Classic anthropological research consisted of participant-observation, data collection, and cultural description, and all these practices presumed an outside position.[26] According to that mode of cultural representation, the detached observer kept a distance to ensure neutrality and impartiality in scientific description. Anthropologists believed that the observer's detachment produced an objective account of social reality. The irony, of course, was that social scientists seldom considered whether their presence as outsiders influenced the behavior of the group under study. Recent studies in cultural anthropology reveal that many of them underestimated the creativity of the people.[27] Anthropologists never imagined that local cultures or minority groups had the audacity to fool them. They failed to recognize that communities performed for the people who studied them.

Américo Paredes, on the other hand, felt that only through participation in a local culture could a more global or objective vision of society be achieved in anthropological research. He argued the issue of representation from an inside position—within the Mexico-Tejano people—to juxtapose it with the "official" or dominant culture at large. Paredes insistently sought to place the folk poets of his culture on the same level of importance as the intellectuals of other cultures, specifically those of Mexico and the United States. He felt the need to reinterpret the image, culture, and history of the Mexican American people, and his unique situation between North American and Mexican society, the social sciences and the humanities, and that of a scholar and folk performer revolutionized the study of culture.

Paredes explored the Mexican American's social reality from a number of positions (literary, musical, and anthropological) rather than remaining locked into one specific point of view. He frequently compared and contrasted the Mexican and North American cultures and allowed the Mexican American people to speak for themselves on their own terms. The performance-oriented approach in folklore had a major impact in the field of cultural anthropology. The method challenged traditional concepts of "culture" that characterized it as a fixed, scientific "object."[28] Once Mexican Americans were no longer prefigured as literary objects or understood exclusively as fixed portraits, their voices contested conventional cultural descriptions. Américo Paredes's method involved a shift from the observing eye or visual paradigm in anthropological investigation to that of a transcriber, interpreter, and author of Mexican and Chicano expressive forms. Folklore as performance is similar to cultural anthropology's literary concern with an ethnography that leans more toward the use of expressive voice over simple observation.[29]

Many of the leading contemporary anthropologists such as James Clifford, Michael M. J. Fischer, and George E. Marcus advocate for an ethnography that incorporates various perspectives rather than a single point of view. For these postmodernists, authority in anthropology is broken up into pieces and can no longer be privileged or understood as foundational. They prefer a mix of multiple realities and different viewpoints when writing about culture, and Américo Paredes's prose fits squarely within these recommendations. The Mexico-Tejano scholar not only anticipated the postmodernist critique in anthropology but also may have surpassed it.[30] His polyphonic position actually achieves more than what Clifford or Fischer proposes in that the performer is the analyst, creator, and translator of the cultural act. This reaches a level of heightened reflexivity unavailable to most folklorists and anthropologists.[31] Américo Paredes's approach is not totalizing but contextual, and his writing consists of an interaction of voices, of positioned utterances, where divisions, genres, and identities become blurred.[32] Paredes's prose is simple and accessible, and a characteristic of his ethnographic research involves a play on his own identity. His perspective may be that of a musician, a folklorist, an anthropologist, a literary critic, a Mexican, or a Chicano. There are no boundaries in his efforts to transcend the borders of nations, classes, and cultures even though the U.S.-Mexican border serves as a symbol. As a folk performer and ethnographer, he became a kind of "ventriloquist," or a "polyphonic" who moved between different worlds to capture the multifaceted aspects of Mexican American culture.

Américo Paredes Challenges Traditional Methods in Cultural Anthropology with His Concept of Folklore as Performance

If most Chicano critics agree that "*With His Pistol in His Hand*" exploded the history of Texas and the myth of the Texas Rangers, a similar claim can be made about Américo Paredes's essay "On Ethnographic Work among Minority Groups: A Folklorist's Perspective"(1977) and the field of cultural anthropology. Américo Paredes was already an advocate of a Chicano revisionist movement that dates back to the late 1960s with a series of essays from the anthropologist Octavio Ignacio Romano (1968, 1970) and the sociologist Nick Vaca (1970).[33] Both Romano and Vaca attacked the negative stereotyping of Mexicans by Anglo anthropologists such as William Madsen, Arthur Rubel, Munro Edmonson, and Margaret Clark. Paredes's ideas anticipated Romano and Vaca's criticism of anthropology and the social sciences in the description of native groups. If years earlier he had disapproved of the chauvinism of Anglo outsiders like Walter Prescott Webb and J. Frank Dobie in their analysis of the Mexico-Tejano border folk, he further clarified his folklorist perspective in his 1977 essay "On Ethnographic Work." But instead of merely attacking these social scientists for their poor description of Mexican Americans, Américo Paredes offered solutions to the problem. And from this position, the suspect findings proved to be more a result of ignorance rather than overt racism.[34] For example, Paredes felt that traditional, mainstream ethnography was simply outdated and needed to be revised: "Anthropologists may need to re-examine the argument that they can give us substantially true pictures of a culture by following time-honored methods. And when the group under study is part of one of our own minorities, the situation takes on a good deal of urgency. It was one thing to publish ethnographies about Trobrianders or Kwakiutls half a century ago; it is another to study people who read what you write and are more than willing to talk back."[35] These "time-honored methods" failed to consider issues such as class, gender, sexuality, ethnicity, educational access to higher institutions, or even the privileged position of the ethnographer. In general, these antiquated ethnographies presented their subjects as objects with no meaningful participation in society.

"On Ethnographic Work" is a significant contribution to the field of cultural anthropology, and it is an essay that many scholars have overlooked in their pursuits of a postmodern ethnography. The ethnographic encounter is at the heart of Américo Paredes's work, a meeting that had assumed for too long that informants gave anthropologists straight answers.[36] Paredes had known for some time that the folk poets often performed and jokesters especially loved to catch people off guard. When these verbal artists spotted an outsider, they would play on language and anecdotes depending on the context and situation, as with the folk performances of the real-life Doroteo and the fictional Vicente and Manuel. The folklorist José R. Reyna has documented this cultural behavior among Chicanos in his book *Raza Humor: Chicano Joke Tradition in Texas* (1980). But what sets "On Ethnographic Work" apart from Américo Paredes's earlier fictional and academic writing was his reading of William Hugh Jansen's essay "The Esoteric-Exoteric Factor in Folklore" (1959). Jansen's concept of identity, role-playing, and role-shifting in expressive behavior was important to Paredes's argument because the notion of performance supported Américo's idea with an academic base. Paredes agreed with Jansen's theory that folklore acts as both a unifying force for a group's identity and a divisive force for a group's attitude toward outsiders, and that performance is critical in illustrating and sharing these thoughts. According to Jansen, "the esoteric applies to what one group thinks of itself and what it supposes others think of it. The exoteric is what one group thinks of another and what it thinks that the other group thinks it thinks."[37]

The group's image of itself, and its image of other groups, is reflected in its folklore repertoire. Songs, tales, jests, and the use of names are critical in gauging the feelings and attitudes one group has toward another group. How this folklore expresses intercultural conflict and cooperation is of special interest along the Lower Rio Grande border when one presumes that Mexico-Tejanos and Anglo-Americans are somewhat conscious of each other's stereotypes. Paredes had always been aware of this fact, and he adopted Jansen's analysis. He became one of the first to recognize folklore as performance because he knew that communities perform for the people who are studying them. Thus, Américo Paredes was one of the earliest figures in the postmodern anthropology movement. Again, cultural anthropologists had previously failed to see that minority groups had the guile or wit to fool the people who studied them. Paredes anticipated other point of views in the study of culture.

In his essay, Américo Paredes raised questions about how curious, liberal-minded scholars with honest intentions fail in their efforts to effectively represent a community.[38] He challenged traditional modes of ethnography and analyzed the cultural baggage that anthropologists brought with them in their analysis of culture. Paredes proposed that a true familiarity with any culture demanded a thorough knowledge of its language, folklore, history, and people, and he carefully showed how the encounter between the ethnographer and informant was far more complex than previously acknowledged by folklorists and anthropologists, alike. It was an open invitation for an array of responses, some of which included folklore performances by the informant. The more stressful the situation, the more these personality types resorted to jokes, "or leg-pulling, or circumspection, or playing to stereotypes."[39] To remedy some of these problems with ethnographic description, Paredes suggested more context was needed to properly interpret the material and offered a performance-oriented approach along with an understanding of the ethnographer's "own unstated, consciously rejected prejudices."[40] For Américo Paredes a more self-reflexive critique of culture was needed for better analysis and study of a particular group.

Paredes combined his knowledge of performance factors, like "social identity, situational context, expressive voice, communicative framing and more," to reassess the function of social science research.[41] He seriously examined traditional folklore and anthropological methods, and his critique had wider implications for the politics of culture. Paredes's idea of "expected behavior" versus "observed behavior" in relationship to Mexican stereotypes was especially important.

> When the Chicano is the ingroup and the Anglo the outgroup, a common pair of stereotypes embodying opposite poles of expected behavior are the "stupid, naive, primitive,

> Mexican peon" versus the "charming urbane Spanish *caballero*." Their origins are at the core of the complex relationships that have existed between Mexicans and Anglos for the past 150 years or so. When the Anglo has looked with disfavor upon the Mexican, the Anglo has seen the Mexican as childlike and not endowed with too much intelligence, an excellent source of field labor if you know how to handle him. . . . On the other hand, when the Anglo has wished to flatter the Mexican, the Anglo has looked upon the Mexican as a refined Spanish gentleman.[42]

Paredes was well aware that Mexican Americans many times assumed the Mexican peon persona in joking situations to poke fun at outsiders, and anthropologists, for this reason, needed to be careful not to accept as genuine these types of performances. They may have been too quick to substantiate traditional theories of culture when they assumed informants gave them straight answers or when they framed their questions for expected results. To avoid such mistakes in the interview process, Américo Paredes recommended that these social scientists be fluent in the language, both standard and dialectal, that they know the peoples' folklore traditions, and that they be more careful with their analysis of verbal responses. Paredes's notion of folklore as performance would aid these cultural anthropologists in recognizing specific textual markers found usually in jokes or tales like "'*Oye, saben la de . . .*' (Listen, do you know the one about . . .)" or "'*Ésa está como el que . . .*' (That's like the guy . . .)" or "'*Éste era un hombre . . . ,*' (This was a man . . .)."[43] This kind of knowledge is useful because it can serve as a clue to what may be expected in a particular situation. What's more the content, style, and tone of the performance are of utmost importance because an awareness of these poetic techniques will allow the researcher to differentiate between something that is factual and something that is simply for entertainment purposes.[44] It is the responsibility of the social scientist to be aware of some of these dynamics in the cultural exchange.

A response to this "oppositional" ethnography was witnessed with the publication of numerous anthropological texts that renounced traditional practices and confronted the "crisis in anthropology."[45] A good example is George E. Marcus and Michael M. J. Fischer's *Anthropology as Cultural Critique* (1986). The text is ordered and arranged in terms of materials used and possible solutions to issues of cultural representation. In their preface, for instance, Marcus and Fischer present a general overview of the current problems of representation within cultural anthropology.[46] In the introduction the authors point to Edward W. Said's *Orientalism* (1979) and Derek Freeman's *Margaret Mead and Samoa* (1983) as archetypes of the contemporary criticisms directed toward the discipline of anthropology. Said cites the various genres of writing that were developed to represent people of color; while Freeman's book concerns itself more with the questions the public raised about anthropology's apathy toward offering a cultural critique of itself. If *Orientalism* serves as the model text for anthropology's first premise—the salvaging and representation of cultural forms—*Margaret Mead and Samoa* stresses the debate of the discipline's other front—to serve as a method of self-reflexive criticism. Both texts appear to be used more as "props" or samples than solutions for the essays that follow; neither actually addresses the problems it raises. The two books merely lay out the dilemma in the social sciences.

George E. Marcus and Michael M. J. Fischer cite numerous texts and offer various examples to illustrate the origins, trends, and problems of anthropology's "experimental moment" and also offer possible solutions. They might have been well served by the work of Américo Paredes. Their "effort[s] at clarifying the present situation of cultural and social anthropology" coincide with many concerns and ideas raised by the Mexico-Tejano folklorist.[47] In fact, Marcus and Fischer propose many of the same alternatives for more accurate ethnographic work suggested earlier by Américo Paredes as possible "experimentations." The issues presented throughout *Anthropology as Cultural Critique*, such as preparation in the discipline, generalizations about cultures, culture as a category of resistance, the complex encounter between ethnographer and subject, and perpetuation of stereotypes, are the same arguments cited by Américo Paredes in his article "On Ethnographic Work." The following excerpts from Marcus and Fischer's text and Paredes's essay illustrate this important point along with a principal reason for the crisis in anthropology.

> One of the most significant processes that has subverted the inclination to find the pristine in fieldwork has been the adaptation of peoples who have been long-term subjects of anthropological interest to anthropologists themselves and their habitual rhetorics. . . . Those peoples who in particular have become classic anthropological subjects, . . . know their status well, and have, with some ambivalence, assimilated anthropological knowledge about them as part of their sense of themselves. Apocryphal stories abound in professional folklore about the American Indian informant who, in response to the ethnographer's question, consults the work of Alfred Kroeber, or the African villager in the same situation who reaches for his copy of Meyer Fortes. The cogent irony in these stories can no longer be received merely as folklore by anthropologists who approach their isolated communities and cultures, not as complete strangers, but as known types.[48]

Marcus and Fischer recognize that too much can be taken for granted by the ethnographer when the informant is aware of outsiders. These people may revert to common stereotypes that they think anthropologists hold about them, which can lead to misrepresentations, not to mention distorted ethnographic research. Thus, Marcus and Fischer stress the need for alternative methods in undertaking fieldwork along with different strategies for writing to rectify the predicament confronted by the human sciences.

Américo Paredes, on the other hand, grew up among the border Mexican poets and he himself was an interpreter of folklore forms. These performers of folklore sang corridos, told legends, and could entertain audiences with their tongue-in-cheek commentaries. As a performer, ethnographer, folklorist, Mexican, and Chicano, Paredes played with his identity as an insider and outsider to describe the Mexico-Tejano culture. He pointed out that verbal artists (in many ways like himself) were very much aware of Anglo stereotypes about them as Mexicans. "A performer assumes the role of the dumb hick for the amusement of people very much like himself. His performance, in fact, involves double role-casting: himself as the hick and his auditors as the type of people (outsiders) who would consider the *ranchero* stupid. . . . The 'I'm just a poor, dumb Mexican peon' persona is a favorite with the border Mexican jokester, who can use it for plain fun among his own group . . . or work it on outsiders with a barbed intent."[49] Once again, the traditional subjects' perceptions of themselves are based on what they believe outsiders think of them. A key factor in ethnographic representation, consequently, can be highly unreliable. I suggest that strong evidence supports the idea that many of the solutions offered in Marcus and Fischer's *Anthropology as Cultural Critique* concur with Paredes's essay "On Ethnographic Work among Minority Groups" and, to some extent, his book "*With His Pistol in His*

Hand." The two anthropologists state toward the end of their book, however, that they are unfamiliar with Paredes's work.[50] In any case, Américo Paredes was an influential cultural anthropologist of his time and his essay "On Ethnographic Work" is a uniquely meritorious document in the field of the social sciences.

Américo Paredes Turns His Attention South of the Border

Recognizing how the border folk poets defended their identity and way of life when they mocked what they felt outsiders thought about them as Mexican Americans, Paredes began to apply this approach in his own writing. This time, however, Paredes turned his attention south of the border to criticize Mexican intellectuals for their insensitive descriptions of Chicanos. Américo Paredes decided to share his views about Mexicans since for some time they had written candidly about what they thought of Mexican Americans.

The book most often cited by Latin American critics as Octavio Paz's best work, *El Laberinto de la Soledad* (1950, rev. 1959), was the text most condemned by Américo Paredes. In nine essays that attempt to synthesize the Mexican culture and people (Paz later stated it was an exercise in "criticism"), the Mexican poet and Nobel laureate drew some extraordinary conclusions with reference to the Mexican character.[51] Octavio Paz's views about machismo and Chicanos and his commentary on the 1968 massacre in Tlatelolco infuriated the Mexico-Tejano anthropologist.[52] Américo Paredes disagreed with the idea that the Mexican *machista* attitude was an Oedipus complex that began as a result of the Spanish-Indian conquest. Here is what Octavio Paz had to say about the Mexican *macho* in his chapter titled "The Sons of *La Malinche*."

> A psychologist would say that resentment is the basis of his character. It would not be difficult to perceive certain homosexual inclinations also, such as the use and abuse of the pistol, a phallic symbol which discharges death rather than life, and the fondness for exclusively masculine guilds. . . . It is impossible not to notice the resemblance between the figure of the *macho* and that of the Spanish conquistador. This is the model—more mythical than real—that determines the images the Mexican people form of men in power: caciques, feudal lords, hacienda owners, politicians, generals, captains of industry. They are all *machos, chingones*.[53]

To which Paredes responded:

> Any evaluation of Mexican *machismo* will not be complete if the following point is ignored: The fundamental attitudes on which *machismo* is based (and which have caused so much distress to those wishing to psychoanalyze the Mexican) are almost universal. . . . There is no evidence that *machismo* (in the exaggerated forms that have been studied and condemned in Mexicans) even existed in Mexico before the Revolution. Available evidence suggests that it is a phenomenon dating from the 1930s to the present, that is to say, from the period after the Revolution.[54]

Américo Paredes felt that machismo was simply courage commemorated in the folk songs of all nations, a noble ideal in any time and any country. He did not accept it as an inherent complex peculiar to the Mexican male as did other social scientists like Vicente Mendoza and Samuel Ramos. This is not to suggest that

Octavio Paz would not have agreed with Paredes's views, or that a poetic license should not be allowed to writers. But what was clear to Paredes was Paz's experimentation as an amateur anthropologist or psychologist at the expense of young Mexican Americans.

Américo Paredes's criticism of Octavio Paz, however, did not stop with the inherent Mexican complex of machismo. Paredes also criticized the Mexican intellectual (along with Capt. E. Duran Ayres of the Los Angeles police force) for his description of Mexican Americans in Los Angeles.[55] In "The Pachuco and Other Extremes" Paz's concern was not to investigate or discuss the *pachuco*'s previous subjection to beatings and other persecutions at the time of the 1942–43 zoot-suit riots; the Mexican poet, instead, was more interested in describing the young Chicano as a "delinquent," "contemptuous," and "perverted" individual.[56] Paz also described the *pachuco* as "an impassive sinister *clown* whose purpose is to cause terror instead of laughter."[57] The Chicano of East L.A. was a sadist and masochist who sought a kind of "painful self-satisfaction" from provoking Anglo society. Again, for Américo Paredes the negative description of Mexican Americans was problematic. He did not see this type of narration as different from what earlier North Americans had written about Mexican and Mexican Americans, only this time around it came from the other side of the border. Paz was a learned individual, in a position to call attention to the problems of young Chicanos in the United States. Instead he elected to avoid the issue altogether, saying that it "is not important to examine the causes of this conflict, and even less so to ask whether or not it has a solution."[58] Rather than describe a bright future for these young Angelenos, the Nobel laureate brought up the past in order to understand the behavior of Mexican Americans living in the United States. He had failed to understand them as Chicanos in the City of Angels.[59]

On the night of October 30, 1969, Américo Paredes was in attendance when Octavio Paz delivered the Hackett Memorial Lecture in Batts Hall at the University of Texas, Austin.[60] In "Mexico: The Last Decade," the honored Mexican speaker, in his address to a young Texas audience, assigned blame for the Massacre of Tlatelolco. It was not a case of "overreaction" by the Mexican government, who responded with brute force to the confusion and disorder created from the student movement. According to Paz, Mexican biology was to blame.[61] Paz's obsession with masks led him to believe the massacre had "correspondences with the Mexican past, especially with the Aztec world, [which was] fascinating, overpowering, and repelling."[62] Behind the *tapado* (the unrevealed presidential candidate) was the Aztec priest with a bloody obsidian knife.

Octavio Paz's commentary offended Américo Paredes because the Chicano scholar was often reminded, growing up in Texas, of the Mexican's so-called bloody nature.[63] Years later, he remembered Octavio Paz's observations and compared them with the folk poets along the border to make a point in an essay titled "The Problem of Identity in a Changing Culture." "If I have given some space to Paz and his fondness for masked figures, it has not been out of mere captiousness but in the hope of making a point. It is worth noting that even intellectuals may indulge in self-derogatory stereotypes, all for the sake of art, of course. But the anonymous Mexican American who creates still another self-derogatory joke is an artist, too. I doubt that any one of us would want to charge Paz with racism. He does get carried away now and then by his fascination with the bloodier aspects of the pre-Columbian cultures."[64] Paredes thought that stereotypes were stereotypes, and there should be no distinction between a scholarly address that conceals inner biases and the indirect insults performed by folk artists. If anything, much more understanding should be expected from the artist-intellectual than say, for example, an ordinary folk performer with little or no education.

The writings of the first secretary of public education in Mexico came under Paredes's scrutiny as well. Despite José Vasconcelos's firsthand experience as a child in Piedras Negras, with the hostile environment along the border, and despite his defense many years later of the Hispanic culture against U.S. intrusion, the Mexican intellectual received some strong criticism from Américo Paredes.[65] Aside from using the names *pocho* ("white-washed" Mexican) and *bárbaros* (barbarians) in his autobiography, *La Tormenta* (1937), Vasconcelos did attempt to direct attention to the problems of Mexicans in the United States.[66] In fact, Vasconcelos seriously considered developing a program to bring these people back to Mexico.[67] These gestures did not seem to convince Américo Paredes, however. As he understood it, Vasconcelos's interest was not sincere because he changed his mind completely after writing his book *La raza cósmica* (1925). He later referred to it as *la raza cómica*, according to Paredes.[68] Moreover, when Mexican Americans truly needed him the most, Vasconcelos deserted under fire, so to speak. During the Mexican Revolution of 1910, he expressed no concern over the slaughter of hundreds of defenseless Mexican peasants by the rural police in south Texas. This indifference was in spite of the help Vasconcelos received from the Mexican American people in the United States during his escape. José Vasconcelos saw the atrocities committed against Mexican Americans as a plot by Venustiano Carranza to sell the Republic of Mexico to the United States.[69] According to Américo Paredes, the Mexican's concern for Chicanos was simply political.

At least two reasons can explain Paredes's criticism of these two Mexican nationals. First, there is the matter of stereotypes. Paredes was extremely sensitive toward any further negative representations of Mexican Americans, from either side of the border. He believed that if these intellectuals had no positive labels to use, then it was best not to employ any at all. Second, the Mexico-Tejano agreed with William Hugh Jansen's theory in "The Esoteric-Exoteric Factor in Folklore" that folklore functions as a unifying force for a group's uniqueness and a disruptive force for a group's feelings toward outsiders. He expressed this idea in a 1996 interview when asked to recall his acceptance speech of El Orden del Aguila Azteca. Paredes chuckled and remarked: "Yes, I was not going to miss the opportunity of telling them [Mexicans] what we thought of them because of what they think of us."[70] In other words, it was a way for Américo Paredes to defend and reaffirm the positive character, culture, and identity of Mexican Americans, who until recent times have lacked the support of Mexican scholars.

Setting New Standards in Ethnography and Folklore

Américo Paredes's performance-oriented approach that illustrates the human potentialities of people and exposes some of the naive practices of ethnographers reaches its culmination with his book *Uncle Remus con chile* (1993). The book offers 217 texts of verbal lore that reflect the attitudes of Mexicans and Texas Mexicans along the Lower Rio Grande border, particularly toward Anglo-Americans. As a postmodern anthropologist, Américo Paredes felt that another point of view was essential. The bulk of the material was collected between 1962 and 1963 in the Lower Rio Grande border region, Chicago, Indiana, and central Mexico. The folklore data are written in English, Spanish, and "Spanglish" as it was performed by the informants.

In addition to the collection of jests and anecdotes about intercultural conflict (in all its dimensions) between Mexicans,

Anglo-Americans, Texas Mexicans, and Mexican Americans, the index of informants is especially interesting. It is broken down into ethnicity, ages, occupations and experiences, gender, and notes of special interest. Texas Mexican males as narrators dominate the list, some twenty-six, although other male groups are included: seven border Mexicans, four Mexicans, three Mexican Americans, an Anglo-Texan, and even a "U.S. painter" whose ethnicity is not mentioned. The women informants consist of two Mexicans, a Texas Mexican, an Anglo-Texan, and a Jewish American. The ages of the performers range from twenty-nine to seventy-seven. The experiences and occupations of these informants include rancher, lawyer, teacher, school principal, judge, WWII and Korean war veterans, barber, wholesale candy salesman, taxi driver, and gas station serviceman. More colorful activities include a former *sedicioso* (seditionist) from the Mexico-Tejano uprisings in 1915 and an occasional small-time smuggler. Among the informants are an amateur historian, a blind man, a nephew of Gregorio Cortez, and a border Mexican who is an excellent performer of deadpan humor. Stereotyped images of Mexicans are no longer justified. Paredes's unique approach toward the data collection of folklore from these groups has caused a reassessment of the functions of orality, ethnicity, and importance of ethnographic composition.

An introductory narrative on the abuses of the Texas Rangers sets the stage for one of the principal reasons for interethnic conflict between Anglo-Americans and Mexico-Tejanos as revealed in *Uncle Remus con chile*.[71] The texts in the collection then move in a variety of directions, such as Anglo women's loose morals and jests about gringos, *mojados* (wetbacks), *agringados* ("white-washed" Mexicans) and machos, closing with the Texas Mexican's attitude toward Anglo-Americans. If ethnographers were quick to accept as genuine the informant's persona that most nearly corresponded with their own unstated biases or prejudices, Américo Paredes subverted the fieldwork of ethnography. He allowed the informants to speak for themselves, on their own terms. For example, in text number thirty-one ("La Discriminación"), informant number fifty (a Texas Mexican male) deliberately misinterpreted a question concerning "discrimination." "Andaban haciendo un 'survey' en el estado de Tejas, para ver si había discriminación en las escuelas. Y le escriben al superintendente de las escuelas de Rio Grande City. Que si había discriminación en sus escuelas. And he answered, 'There is no discrimination down here. We treat Anglos just like everybody else.'"[72]

There are other examples throughout the book, some vulgar, others quite sexist, and still others extremely racist. But Américo Paredes made a point with his recorded texts. If Mexican Americans historically had been the objects of criticism with no voice, as an ethnographer he allowed them to speak for themselves. Since the study of culture is a two-way street, it cannot be studied, shaped, and framed from only one angle. No matter how subtle and objective a perspective may appear to be, the analysis of culture involves an interaction between at least two groups. Culture for Américo Paredes was fluid and multifaceted as the anthropologist Renato Rosaldo pointed out. "He sees culture as bound by circumstances, constantly changing, and internally diverse. [Paredes's] goal is, not totalizing, but contextualist. Rather than delineate a static pattern, he shows the interplay of culture, power, and history. When one asks for example, about so-called ethnic labels of self-identification . . . Paredes counters like a fox, not with a single 'self-designation,' but with myriad names. It all depends, he says, on who is speaking to whom under what circumstances. Are they distant or intimate? Is the relationship egalitarian or one of dominance and subordination?"[73] These recent techniques in ethnography show that Américo Paredes was ahead of his time in theory and practice and that the postmodern movement in cultural anthropology would profit from a serious consideration of his contributions. As Víctor J. Guerra states, "He effectively challenged prevailing theoretical notions and was instrumental in setting new methodological standards for ethnographers. He is credited with ushering in some of the key techniques and concepts that would later constitute reflexive and postmodern ethnography and folkloristics."[74] Paredes's talents as a Mexican American writer, musician, and scholar privileged him as a social scientist. Few cultural anthropologists of his time possessed this type of ability and versatility, and his work revealed the "liberating power of folklore study" and its essential relationship with the writing of culture.[75] His unique situation in la frontera in many ways achieves more than what has been suggested by some cultural anthropologists. Paredes demonstrated in his work that the folk poet is the psychoanalyst, the maker, and the interpreter of the cultural act, and this recognition allows a level of heightened reflexivity unavailable to most folklorists and anthropologists. This personal experience of multidimensionality—simultaneously a subject and an observer, a performer and a scholar, a bilingual man of la frontera—would lead to a complex awareness of what is now understood as the postmodern. In reality, though, Paredes's location between cultures and languages was more than a simple rejection of the modernist paradigm in cultural anthropology. It became a way of life for Mexican Americans, and Américo Paredes expressed these tensions and contradictions in his life and work as a folk poet of his people.

Conclusion

When Américo Paredes wrote his most famous book, *"With His Pistol in His Hand,"* border culture was considered backward and insignificant, impure, the outcome of miscegenation. This belief served as justification for Anglo dominance over the Mexican people, and it was supported, perpetuated, and made legitimate throughout the American Southwest. Américo rejected this idea and argued that a mestizo culture—a fusion of different groups—was emerging in south Texas before it was interrupted by the westward expansion of the United States. He challenged those scholars who had portrayed his people in a negative light, and his writings helped shape a positive cultural identity for Mexican Americans. All his life, Américo Paredes insisted that a distinctive culture evolved when the North American and Mexican cultures mingled and clashed along the Lower Rio Grande region. This new culture was born when the Mexican American people resisted cultural assimilation and affirmed their rights as a people. It became the Mexican American people's resolve *de no dejarse* (not to allow it), not to give in to the injustices suffered at the hands of foreigners.

I argue that Américo Paredes's concept of folklore as performance resonated in much of his literary and scholarly writings. These items of folklore consisted of both overt and subtle signs that expressed the tension and resentment between Anglos and Mexico-Tejanos. This notion of performance went against traditional perspectives in folklore and anthropology because it offered another point of view in the study of culture. In Paredes's works, Mexican Americans were allowed to express their views of what they thought about others. Rather than ask what Mexican Americans are, Américo Paredes asked what it meant to be a Mexican American. This approach turned cultural studies upside down because it revealed the interplay of culture, power, and history in Texas discourse. The Mexico-Tejano scholar and folk poet was increasingly aware of the power relations that existed along the Lower Rio Grande border region, and his analysis of the performances in specific situations revealed the hostility and contradictions experienced by a people under domination. He approached the Mexican American culture from a variety of perspectives—literary, musical, and anthropological—in an effort to understand the multifaceted nature of the Spanish-speaking people of Greater Mexico. His revisionist efforts criticized both North American and Mexican scholars—including Walter Prescott Webb, J. Frank Dobie, Octavio Paz, and José Vasconcelos—for their narrow-minded views toward Mexican Americans.

Some forty years after its publication, "*With His Pistol in His Hand*" continues to speak to a new generation of Mexicans and Mexican Americans. One cannot study the history of Texas without mentioning this book; folklorists and cultural anthropologists have benefited from Paredes's concept of folklore as performance; literary critics recognize that often the best stories are those that are found in oral tradition; and ethnomusicologists have learned a great deal from Paredes's knowledge of Mexican and Mexican American folk music. The book is now in its fourteenth printing (2004), and that achievement is due in large part to the text's scholarly rigor, simple and straightforward prose, cross-disciplinary perspective, and groundbreaking work in Chicano cultural studies.

One criticism of Américo Paredes's revisionist efforts is that women seldom had a voice in this traditional and patriarchal culture; yet Paredes was a product of his time. Nonetheless, the landscape of academic research has changed considerably with regard to the importance of and attitudes toward minority groups, and scholars like Américo Paredes contributed enormously toward this understanding. His knowledge of border culture—with its fluidity and multifaceted nature—has become a source of inspiration for many writers and scholars in their efforts to expose and reinterpret the traditional "borders" of class, gender, and sexuality. For instance, Gloria Anzaldúa's well-known work *Borderlands/La Frontera: The New Mestiza* (1987) explores the reality of Mexican and Chicana women along the Lower Rio Grande border. Like Paredes, she uses such disciplines as anthropology, folklore, literature, history, and music to locate Chicanas within the dominant cultural models of the United States and Mexico. Anzaldúa makes it clear that mestizas have a different worldview as she rewrites the stories of Mexican females, past and present. Her recovery project leads to a social, geographical, and political awareness that Anzaldúa calls a "new *mestiza* consciousness," a feminist knowledge. Américo Paredes examined in his lifetime a particular experience of Mexican Americans, especially that of males; Anzaldúa explores the potentiality of *la mujer chicana* at the turn of the twenty-first century. Culture can no longer be understood as static or fixed. *Chicana Traditions: Continuity and Change* (2002), edited by Norma E. Cantú and Olga Nájera-Ramírez, is another text that merits consideration.

Thematically speaking, violent cultural conflict between Mexicans and North Americans is now a limited concept. Notions of "transnationalism," "globalization," and "*sin fronteras*" are now the theories of choice to understand the blending of ideas and cultures, a sort of worldwide syncretism, or *mestizaje*. Américo Paredes anticipated these ideas in his work, too, with his across-the-border methods. In fact, late in his career many of his courses were cross-listed in the ethnic studies, Mexican American studies, and Latin American studies programs. And as he suggested in his 1940 semiautobiographical novel *George Washington Gómez*, the Mexican American middle class will play a pivotal role in the shaping of culture, trends, and policies throughout the United States, and these ideas will influence Mexico and Latin America more generally. The celebrations of *el 16 de septiembre* and *cinco de mayo* in the United States along with the spirit of mariachi music throughout the world are examples of these border crossings. Other cultures have followed a similar path to create a society in the U.S. that "knows no borders."

Today, Paredes's creative writings, correspondence, syllabi, calendars, teaching notes, diaries, sketches, legal documents, financial records, sound recordings, photographic material, and other artifacts are inventoried at the Nettie Lee Benson Latin American Collection at the University of Texas at Austin. The Américo Paredes Center for Cultural Studies (formerly the Center for Intercultural Studies in Folklore and Ethnomusicology) is an interdisciplinary center dedicated to the creation and diffusion of cultural studies scholarship and research. In addition, "Mariachi Paredes de Tejastitlán," founded at UT Austin in 1976–77, keeps his memory alive with traditional Mexican music at various events. Américo Paredes's most notable awards and honors include the Guggenheim Fellowship in 1962, the first endowed professorship in his discipline in 1983, the Américo Paredes Distinguished Lecture Series established in 1987, the Charles Frankel Award from the National Endowment for the Humanities in 1989, the Order of the Aztec Eagle from Mexico in 1991, recognition by the American Folklore Society as the most important scholar in Mexican, Caribbean, and Latin American folklore in 1997, a Lifetime Achievement Award from the Texas Book Festival in 1998, and the Américo Paredes Middle School named in his honor in 1998.

In the late 1990s the Center for Mexican American Books at the University of Texas at Austin published two of his early short stories, "Mi Tía Pilar" and "Mr. White," in *Reflexiones: New Directions in Mexican American Studies*. The first tale deals with a mother who shoots at her son-in-law for physically abusing his wife, and the latter is about a black father (Mr. White) who moves into the vacated house of a retired Texas Ranger, awaiting his return for shooting his son. To my knowledge, Américo Paredes's acceptance speech for the Order of the Aztec Eagle Award in 1991 has not been published.

Américo and Amelia Paredes had three children, Alan, Vicente, and Julia, grandchildren, and great-grandchildren. Amelia managed the household, assisted individuals diagnosed with the same condition as her daughter, and became a prominent advocate for the rights of the developmentally disabled in Texas. Américo Paredes publicly acknowledged the importance of Amelia's role in his professional accomplishments. Amelia passed away in July 1999, two months after her husband. Paredes's son from a previous marriage, Américo Jr., lives in Brownsville, Texas; his other children live in Austin.

One final story sheds some light on Américo Paredes in his later years. A well-known musician in Austin, Texas, had searched for a song that her mother, María del Refugio Coronado-Zamudio—better known as "Cuquita"—used to sing. Rummaging through sheet music and record stores for about a year, Tish Hinojosa was unable to find the ballad "Collar the Perlas" (A Necklace of Pearls).[1]

One day, Hinojosa received a call from someone who said he might know of the song that she had been searching for, although he knew it under a different title, "Déjame Llorar" (Let Me Cry).

The individual offered to sing it for her at his home. Tish Hinojosa went to the man's home and was serenaded by none other than Américo Paredes as he played his classical guitar and sang with "his aging but clear voice."[2] Deeply moved, Hinojosa at that moment began an apprenticeship with Don Américo, learning the corridos, *boleros*, and anecdotes of days gone by. She later dedicated a song to the Paredes family, "Con Su Pluma en Su Mano" (With His Pen in His Hand), on her album *Frontejas* (1994).

This is the story of Américo Paredes and the impact he had on the lives of those around him. I hope that this book in some small way will contribute to his legacy so that others will be inspired as I have been by his teachings, scholarship, and music. I have learned that integrity and inspiration, theory and practice, life and work are not separated or divorced from daily life—not simply things to be appreciated and contemplated in the abstract. Thoughts and manners were one and the same for Américo Paredes, and we should try to follow his example in our daily lives and professional careers.

Notes

Chapter 1

1. Américo Paredes, dedication in *"With His Pistol in His Hand": A Border Ballad and Its Hero* (Austin: University of Texas Press, 1958).

2. Richard Bauman, *Story, Performance, and Event: Contextual Studies of Oral Narrative* (New York: Cambridge University Press, 1986).

3. Vito Alessio Robles, *Monterrey en la historia y en la leyenda* (México: Antigua Librería Robredo de José Porrúa e Hijos, 1936), 98.

4. Seymour B. Liebman, *The Jews in New Spain: Faith, Flame, and the Inquisition* (Coral Gables, Fla.: University of Miami Press, 1970), 142.

5. Ibid., 148.

6. Alonso de León, *Historia de Nuevo León*, ed. Israel Cavazos Garza. Monterrey: Gobierno del Estado de Nuevo León, 1961, 54.

7. Martin A. Cohn, *The Martyr: The Story of a Secret Jew and the Mexican Inquisition in the Sixteenth Century* (Philadelphia: Jewish Publication Society of America, 1973), 110.

8. A. León, 54–55.

9. V. A. Robles, 112.

10. S. B. Liebman, 150.

11. A. León, 55.

12. Alejandro Prieto, *Historia, Geografía y Estadística del Estado de Tamaulipas* (Mexico, 1873, reproducción facsimilar de la edición de 1873, S.A. Librería, México, D.F.: Manuel Porrúa, 1949), 92–110.

13. Vicente de Santa María, *Relación Histórica de la Colonia del Nuevo Santander* (México: Universidad Nacional Autónoma de México Dirección General de Publicaciones, 1973), 75.

14. A. Prieto, 194–95.

15. Lawrence Francis Hill, *José de Escandón and the Founding of Nuevo Santander: A Study in Spanish Colonization* (Columbus: Ohio University Press, 1926), 59.

16. Ibid., 60.

17. Ibid., 66.

18. Ibid., 67.

19. A. Paredes, *"With His Pistol in His Hand,"* 9.

20. Ibid., 11.

21. Ibid., 10.

22. Ibid., 9, 15.

23. Pike, Zebulon M., *The Expeditions of Zebulon Montgomery Pike, To Headwaters of the Mississippi River, Through Louisiana Territory, and in New Spain, during the Years 1805–6–7*, ed. Elliot Coues (New York: Francis P. Harper, 1895), 2:797.

24. T. R. Ferehnbach, *Lone Star: A History of Texas and the Texans* (New York: Macmillan, 1968), 135.

25. Ibid., 452.

26. Rodolfo Acuña, *Occupied America: A History of Chicanos*. 3rd ed. (New York: Harper Collins, 1988), 7.

27. Eugene C. Barker, *Mexico and Texas* (Austin: University of Texas Press, 1934), 149.

28. Raymund, A. Paredes, "The Origins of Anti-Mexican Sentiment in the United States," in *New Directions in Chicano Scholarship*, ed. Ricardo Romo and Raymund Paredes, 139–65 (San Diego: Regents of the University of California, 1978).

29. Mary Austin Holley, *Texas: Observations, Historical, Geographical, and Descriptive* (1833; rpt., Austin, 1935), 128.

30. Raymund A. Paredes, "The Mexican Image in American Travel Literature, 1831–1869," *New Mexico Historical Review* (1977): 6.

31. Antonio López de Santa Anna, "Manifesto Relative to His Operations in the Texas Campaign and His Capture," in *The Mexican Side of the Texas Revolution*, trans. and notes Carlos E. Castañeda, 17 (Austin: Graphic Ideas, 1970).

32. I. J. Cox, "The Southwest Boundary of Texas," *Southwest Historical Quarterly* 1, no. 2 (October 1902): 91.

33. Walter Prescott Webb, *The Texas Rangers: A Century of Frontier Defense* (Boston: Houghton, Mifflin, 1935), 84–86.

34. Richard Griswold del Castillo, *The Treaty of Guadalupe Hidalgo: A Legacy of Conflict* (Norman and London: University of Oklahoma Press, 1990), 4.

35. General Winfield Scott, *Memoirs*. 2 Vols (New York: Sheldon Publishers, 1864).

36. Charles W. Goldfinch, *The Mexican American* (New York: Arno Press, 1974), 12.

37. David Montejano, *Anglos and Mexicans in the Making of Texas, 1836–1986* (Austin: University of Texas Press, 1987), 37.

38. Jovita González, "Social Life in Cameron, Starr and Zapata Counties" (master's thesis, University of Texas at Austin, 1930), 27, 58.

39. Emilio C. Forto, "Actual Situation on the River Rio Grande." *Pan American Labor Press*, September 11, 1918, 3.

40. D. Montejano, 113.

41. James Sandos, *Rebellion in the Borderlands: Anarchism and the Plan of San Diego, 1904–1923* (Norman and London: University of Oklahoma Press, 1992), 71.

42. Ibid., 72.

43. Ibid., 81. See also Benjamin Heber Johnson, *Revolution in Texas: How a Forgotten Rebellion and Its Bloody Suppression Turned Mexicans into Americans* (New Haven and London: Yale University Press, 2003), 72.

44. E. C. Forto, 4.

45. Charles C. Cumberland, "Border Raids in the Lower Rio Grande Valley—1915," *Southwestern Historical Quarterly* 57, no. 3 (January 1954): 301.

46. W. P. Webb, *The Texas Rangers*, 478.

47. B. H. Johnson, 120.

48. C. Cumberland, 300.

49. Frank C. Pierce, *A Brief History of the Lower Rio Grande Valley* (Wisconsin: George Banta, 1917), 115.

50. B. H. Johnson, 3.

51. Cecil Robinson, *With Ears of Strangers: The Mexican in American Literature* (Tucson: University of Arizona Press, 1963).

52. W. P. Webb, *The Texas Rangers*, 17.

53. Noah Smithwick, *the Evolution of a State; or, Recollections of Old Texas Days* (1900; rpt. Austin: Steck-Vaughn, 1968), 130; John Russell Bartlett, *Personal Narrative of explorations and incidents in Texas, New Mexico, California, Sonora, and Chihuahua connected with the United States and Mexican Boundary Commission during the years 1850, '51, '52, and '53* (1854; rpt. Chicago: Rio Grande Press, 1965), 2:74; William Madsen, *The Mexican American of South Texas* (New York: Holt, Rinehart and Winston, 1964).

54. William Wells Newell, "The Study of Folklore," *Transactions of the New York Academy of Sciences* 9 (1890): 134–36.

55. James Charles McNutt, "Beyond Regionalism: Texas Folklorists and the Emergence of a Post Regional Consciousness" (Ph.D. diss., University of Texas at Austin, 1982), 324–25.

56. Ibid., 325, 329–30.

57. Homi K. Bhabha, *The Location of Culture* (London and New York: Routledge, 1994), 66.

58. J. Frank Dobie, ed., *Publications of the Texas Folk-Lore Society* (Austin, 1925), 4:10–43.

59. Ibid., 4:30–43.

60. Américo Paredes, "El folklore de los grupos de origen mexicano en los Estados Unidos," *Folklore Americano* 14 (1966): 146–63. See also Américo Paredes,

Folklore and Culture on the Texas-Mexican Border, ed. Richard Bauman (Austin: CMAS Books, 1993), 3–18.

61. J. Frank Dobie, ed., *Puro Mexicano* (Dallas: Southern Methodist University Press, 1935), 10–13.

62. Ibid.

63. J. Manuel Espinosa, "Major Stages in the Development of Espinosa's Folklore Studies," in Aurelio M. Espinosa, *The Folklore of Spain in the American Southwest*, ed. J. Manuel Espinosa, 29 (Norman and London: University of Oklahoma Press, 1985).

64. Aurelio M. Espinosa, "Spanish and Spanish-American Folk Tales," *Journal of American Folklore* 64 (1951): 151.

65. Aurelio M. Espinosa, "New Mexican Spanish Folklore: Part 2, Myths; Part 2, Superstitions and Beliefs," *Journal of American Folklore* 23 (1910): 395.

66. Aurelio M. Espinosa, "New Mexican Spanish Folklore: Part 3, Folktales, *Journal of American Folklore* 24 (1911): 398, 423.

67. J. Manuel Espinosa, "Espinosa's New Mexican Background and Professional Career," in A. Espinosa, *The Folklore of Spain*, 17.

68. A. Paredes, "El folklore de los grupos de origen mexicano en Estados Unidos," 147.

69. Arthur L. Campa, "Juan de Oñate Was Mexican: The Coronado Cuarto Centennial and the Spaniards," in *Arthur L. Campa and the Coronado Cuarto Centennial*, ed. Anselmo F. Arellano and Julian Josue Vigil, 35 (Las Vegas, N. Mex.: Editorial Telerana, 1980).

70. Arthur L. Campa, "The Spanish Folksong in the Southwest," *University of New Mexico Bulletin, Modern Language Series* 1, no. 4 (1933): 7–8.

71. Arthur L. Campa, *Hispanic Culture in the Southwest* (Norman: University of Oklahoma Press, 1979).

72. Arthur L. Campa, *Spanish Folk-Poetry in New Mexico* (Albuquerque: University of New Mexico Press, 1946), 15.

73. Arthur L. Campa, "New Generation," in *Arthur L. Campa and the Coronado Cuarto Centennial*, 25–26.

74. Arthur L. Campa, "Cultural Variations in the Anglo-Spanish Southwest," *Western Review* 7 (Spring 1970): 8–9.

75. Arthur L. Campa, "On the Banks of the Rio Grande," in *Arthur L. Campa and the Coronado Cuarto Centennial*, 11.

76. Leticia Magda Garza-Falcón, *Gente Decente: A Borderlands Response to the Rhetoric of Dominance*. Austin: University of Texas Press, 1998. 75–76.

77. Jovita González, "Social Life in Cameron, Starr, and Zapata Counties" (master's thesis, University of Texas at Austin, 1930), 113.

78. Jovita González, "Tales and Songs of the Texas-Mexicans," in *Man, Bird, and Beast,* 109–11 (Austin: Texas Folk-Lore Society, 1930).

79. Jovita González, "Folk-lore of the Texas-Mexican *Vaquero,*" *Texas and Southwestern Lore* 6 (1927): 22.

80. Jovita González, "America Invades the Border Towns," *Southwest Review* 15 (1930): 470.

81. Ibid., 477.

82. Américo Paredes and Raymund Paredes, eds. *Mexican American Authors* (Boston: Houghton Mifflin, 1972), 8.

83. José E. Limón, *Dancing with the Devil: Society and Cultural Poetics in Mexican-American South Texas* (Madison: University of Wisconsin Press, 1994), 61, 214.

84. A. Paredes, "El folklore de los grupos de origen mexicano en Estados Unidos," 164. See also A. Paredes, *Folklore and Culture,* 18.

Chapter 2

1. A good portion of this chapter is based on two interviews granted by Américo Paredes in Austin, Texas. Juan Gómez-Quiñones, José E. Limón, Teresa McKenna, and Victor Nelson conducted one interview on August 23, 1984. That interview has not been published. Twelve years later, despite Américo Paredes's failing health, Héctor Calderón and I conversed with him at his home on July 13, 1996. See Calderón and Morín, "Interview with Américo Paredes," *Nepantla: Views from South* 1, no. 1 (2000): 197–228.

2. Kimberly García, "Author Battles Racist Views," *Brownsville Herald* (Sunday, August 4, 1991).

3. Juan Gómez-Quiñones, José Limón, Teresa McKenna, and Victor Nelson, interview with Américo Paredes, August 23, 1984, Austin, Tex., copy in author's possession. Translation of the father's comment: This is the one who will do something for us, for our family. He is the one who will go to school.

4. Calderón and Morín, "Interview," 204–205. *Espinela,* an octosyllabic ten-line stanza named after the Spanish poet and musician Vicente Espinel in 1591; *redondilla,* an octosyllabic quatrain; *canto a desafío,* a challenge song, literally "song to challenge."

5. Américo Paredes, "The Undying Love of *El Indio* Córdova," *Ernesto Galarza Commemorative Lecture: Inaugural Lecture, 1986* (Stanford: Stanford Center for Chicano Research, Stanford University, 1987).

6. K. García, "Author Battles Racist Views," *Brownsville Herald.*

7. Gómez-Quiñones, Limón, McKenna, and Nelson, interview, August 23, 1984.

8. Ibid.

9. Calderón and Morín, "Interview," 207.

10. Gómez-Quiñones, Limón, McKenna, and Nelson, interview, August 23, 1984; William Shakespeare, "The Merchant of Venice," *The Globe Illustrated Shakespeare: The Complete Works Annotated*, ed. Howard Staunton, 415 (New York: Gramercy Books, 1979).

11. Gómez-Quiñones, Limón, McKenna, and Nelson, interview, August 23, 1984.

12. Américo Paredes, *Between Two Worlds* (Houston: Arte Público Press, 1991), 24.

13. José E. Limón, *Mexican Ballads, Chicano Poems: History and Influence in Mexican-American Social Poetry* (Berkeley and Los Angeles: University of California Press, 1992), 57–58.

14. A. Paredes, *Between Two Worlds*, 139.

15. Ibid., 26–27.

16. José E. Limón considers it to be Américo Paredes's best poem. See *Mexican Ballads, Chicano Poems*.

17. Merle Simmons, *The Mexican Corrido as a source for Interpretive Study of Mexico (1870–1950)* (Bloomington: Indiana University Press, 1957), 61.

18. Américo Paredes, "Guitarreros," *Southwest Review* (Autumn 1964); see also A. Paredes, *Between Two Worlds*, 29.

19. Rafael Pérez-Torres, *Movements in Chicano Poetry: Against Myths, Against Margins* (New York: Cambridge University Press, 1995), 251.

20. Calderón and Morín, "Interview," 205.

21. Américo Paredes, *Cantos de Adolescencia* (San Antonio: Librería Española, 1937), 3.

22. Ibid., 4.

23. Calderón and Morín, "Interview," 225.

24. Américo Paredes, *George Washington Gómez: A Mexicotexan Novel* (Houston: Arte Público Press, 1990), 270–71.

25. Calderón and Morín, "Interview," 225.

26. Ibid., 216.

27. Rolando Hinojosa, introduction to A. Paredes, *George Washington Gómez*, 5–6.

28. Aristotle, *Poetics*, trans. with an introduction and notes by Gerald F. Else (Ann Arbor: University of Michigan Press, 1970), 53.

29. A. Paredes, *George Washington Gómez*, 184.

30. Ibid., 185.

31. Ibid.

32. Ibid., 186–87.

33. Ibid., 187.

34. Ibid.

35. Ibid., 281–82.

36. Ibid., 295.

37. Ibid., 297.

38. Ibid.

39. Hart Stilwell, introduction to *Border City* (New York: Doubleday and Doran, 1945).

40. Ibid., 52.

41. Rey Guevara Vásquez, "Maverick Scholar Fighting to Correct History's Prejudice," *Austin American-Statesman*, February 7, 1982, C1.

42. According to the 1984 interview, Américo recalled how he obtained the post. The military had discovered that the political editor of the army newspaper at the time was a member of the communist party who had fought with the republicans in Spain. The army released him and, given Paredes's background in journalism, the administration hired him on the spot.

43. Héctor Calderón, "Literatura fronteriza tejana: El compromiso con la historia en Américo Paredes, Rolando Hinojosa y Gloria Anzaldúa," *Mester: Literary Journal of the Graduate Students of the Department of Spanish and Portuguese University of California* 12, 13, no. 2–1 (Fall–Spring 1993–94) : 43.

44. Américo Paredes, "Desde Tokio," *El Universal: El Gran Diario de México*, 17 de junio de 1947.

45. Calderón and Morín, "Interview," 212.

46. Américo Paredes, preface to *The Shadow* (Houston: Arte Público Press, 1998).

47. Américo Paredes to Ed Manning, June 24, 1965, Américo Paredes Papers, 1886–1999, Benson Latin American Collection, General Libraries, University of Texas at Austin; hereafter cited as Paredes Papers.

48. Calderón and Morín, "Interview," 220.

49. Ibid., 226.

50. A. Paredes to Ed Manning, June 24, 1965, Paredes Papers.

51. Ibid.

52. Ibid.

53. Ibid.

54. Américo Paredes to Jim McNutt, 23, June 1982, Paredes Papers.

55. James Charles McNutt, "Beyond Regionalism: Texas Folklorists and the Emergence of a Post-Regional Consciousness" (Ph. D. diss., University of Texas at Austin, 1982), 325.

56. Mody C. Boatright to Tristam Coffin, 13 April 1964, Mody C. Boatright Papers, Center for American History, Archives and Manuscripts, University of Texas at Austin.

57. Richard Bauman, personal communication, August 22, 2002.

58. Américo Paredes, letter of resignation, February 1, 1972, Paredes Papers, 1–4.

59. Ibid., 1–2.

60. David Montejano, "In Memory of Américo Paredes," in Victor J. Guerra, ed., *In Memory of Américo Paredes,* 43 (Center for Mexican American Studies, University of Texas at Austin, May 23, 1999).

61. María Herrera-Sobek, "Américo Paredes: A Tribute," *Mexican Studies/Estudios Mexicanos* 2, no. 16 (2000): 239.

62. Edward W. Said, *Representations of the Intellectual* (New York: Random House, 1994), 3–23.

63. Manuel Peña and Richard Bauman, "Américo Paredes (1915–1999)," *Journal of American Folklore* 113 (Spring 2000): 196.

64. Américo Paredes to Horst de la Croix, April 5, 1986, Paredes Papers.

65. Billy Porterfield, "Twilight of a Great Man: Illness Makes Work Harder for Hispanic UT Scholar, 74," *Austin American-Statesman,* July 28, 1989.

66. Roberto C. González, "A Hero and a Mentor: Américo Paredes' Legacy Lives on in His Works," *Brownsville Herald,* May 19, 1999.

67. Ibid.

68. Beverly Stoeltje, in Guerra, *In Memory of Américo Paredes,* 11.

Chapter 3

1. See, for example, Ramón Saldívar, *Chicano Narrative: The Dialectics of Difference* (Madison: University of Wisconsin Press, 1990), 26–42; Rolando Hinojosa-Smith's comments in "This Writer's Sense of Place," in *The Texas Literary Tradition: Fiction, Folklore, History,* ed. Don Graham et al. (Austin: College of Liberal Arts, University of Texas at Austin, Texas State Historical Association, 1983), 120–24; Tomás Rivera's remarks in Juan Bruce-Novoa, *Chicano Authors: Inquiry by Interview* (Austin: University of Texas Press, 1980), 150; José Limón, "Américo Paredes: A Man from the Border," *Revista Chicano-Riqueña* 8, no. 3 (1980); and Héctor Calderón and José David Saldívar, editors' introduction to *Criticism in the Borderlands: Studies in Chicano Literature, Culture, and Ideology* (Durham and London: Duke University Press, 1991), 1–7.

2. A. Paredes, "*With His Pistol in His Hand,*" 15. See also Daniel D. Arreola, *Tejano South Texas: A Mexican Cultural Province* (Austin: University of Texas Press, 2002), 35.

3. For more information on the folk songs of the Lower Rio Grande Border see Américo Paredes, *A Texas-Mexican Cancionero: Folksongs of the Lower Border* (Urbana: University of Illinois Press, 1976).

4. A. Paredes, "With His Pistol in His Hand," 19.

5. David Montejano, *Anglos and Mexicans in the Making of Texas, 1836–1986* (Austin: University of Texas Press, 1987), 113.

6. A. Paredes, "*With His Pistol in His Hand,*" 108.

7. Ibid., 62.

8. Ibid., 52.

9. Ibid., 94.

10. Ibid., 99.

11. Héctor Calderón, "Reinventing the Border," in *American Mosaic: Multicultural Readings in Context,* ed. Barbara Roche Rico and Sandra Mano, 518 (Boston: Houghton Mifflin, 1995).

12. A. Paredes's "*With His Pistol in His Hand*" is in many ways analogous to the work of the nineteenth-century Argentine writer and poet José Hernández. See J. Hernández, *Martín Fierro* (Buenos Aires: Editorial Universitaria, 1961).

13. A. Paredes, "*With His Pistol in His Hand,*" 149.

14. Ibid.

15. Ibid., 114.

16. Another incident occurred the same year Américo Paredes's doctoral dissertation and essay on the Mexican *corrido* were printed. Américo Paredes published in the *Journal of American Folklore* a two-page review of Merle E. Simmons's book *The Mexican Corrido as a Source of Interpretive Study of Modern Mexico (1870–1950)*. While praising the author for accomplishing "perhaps the first serious study of the Mexican *corrido* to appear in English," he highlighted also the major weaknesses of the book. In discussing these flaws, perhaps due to "hasty" readings, Paredes recommended to future investigators a better knowledge of folk language, ballad conventions, and an "ear for the ballad style." This review initiated a controversy over the origins of the Mexican *corrido* between Américo Paredes and Merle E. Simmons. See Merle E. Simmons, "The Ancestry of Mexico's *Corridos,*" *Journal of American Folklore* 76 (1963); Américo Paredes, "The Ancestry of Mexico's *Corridos:* A Matter of Definitions," *Journal of American Folklore* 76 (1963).

17. Américo Paredes, "The Mexican *Corrido:* Its Rise and Fall," in *Madstones and Twisters*, ed. Moody C. Boatright, Wilson M. Hudson, and Allen Maxwell, 95 (Dallas: Southern Methodist University Press, 1958).

18. Ibid., 104.

19. Raymund Paredes, "The Evolution of Chicano Literature," in *Three American Literatures: Essays in Chicano, Native American, and Asian-American*

Literature for Teachers of American Literature, ed. Houston A. Baker, 51–53 (New York: Modern Language Association of America, 1982).

20. Carey McWilliams, *North from Mexico: The Spanish Speaking People of the United States* (New York: Praeger, 1990), 71

21. Charles F. Lummis, *The Land of Poco Tiempo* (New York: Charles Scribner's Sons, 1893); Lummis, *The Spanish Pioneers* (Chicago: Charles McClurg, 1893); Aurelio Espinosa, *The Folklore of Spain in the American Southwest: Traditional Spanish Folk Literature in Northern New Mexico and Southern Colorado*, ed. J. Manuel Espinosa (Norman and London: University of Oklahoma Press, 1985).

22. Roger D. Abrahams, introduction to *"And Other Neighborly Names": Social Process and Cultural Image in Texas Folklore*, ed. Richard Bauman and Roger D. Abrahams (Austin and London: University of Texas Press, 1981), 5.

23. A. Paredes, introduction to *"With His Pistol in His Hand."*

24. A. Paredes, *"With His Pistol in His Hand,"* 154.

25. John Holmes McDowell, "The *Corrido* of Greater Mexico as Discourse, Music, and Event," in *"And Other Neighborly Names,"* 44–75.

26. Héctor Calderón, "Texas Border Literature: Cultural Transformation and Historical Reflection in the Works of Américo Paredes, Rolando Hinojosa and Gloria Anzaldúa," *Dispositio* 16, no. 41 (1991–92): 25.

27. McDowell, "The *Corrido* of Greater Mexico," 46.

28. Joe Holley, "With His Guitar in His Hand," *Texas Observer*, October 29, 1993, 16–18.

29. Ibid., 18.

30. R. Saldívar, *Chicano Narrative*, 27.

31. José David Saldívar, "Chicano Border Narratives as Cultural Critique," in Calderón and Saldívar, *Criticism in the Borderlands*, 167–80.

32. Ibid., 167.

33. Ibid., 170.

34. George E. Marcus and Michael M. J. Fischer, *Anthropology as Cultural Critique: An Experimental Moment in the Human Sciences* (Chicago: University of Chicago Press, 1986), 8.

35. José E. Limón, *Dancing with the Devil: Society and Cultural Poetics in Mexican-American South Texas* (Madison: University of Wisconsin Press, 1994), 87.

36. Renato Rosaldo, *Culture and Truth: The Remaking of Social Analysis* (Boston: Beacon Press, 1993), 150.

37. Ibid., 151.

38. Héctor Calderón, "Reinventing the Border," in *American Mosaic: Multicultural Readings in Context*, ed. Barbara Roche Rico and Sandra Mano, 2nd ed. (Boston: Houghton Mifflin, 1995), 518.

39. Ibid.

40. Ramón Saldívar, "The Folk Base of Chicano Narrative: Américo Paredes' *With His Pistol in His Hand* and the *Corrido* Tradition" in *Chicano Narrative*, 27.

41. R. Saldívar, *Chicano Narrative*, 27.

42. Tomás Rivera suggested Chicano literature was one of life in search of form. This interpretation entails a search for a way to translate into written form the array of cultural possibilities expressed within the multifaceted, Mexican American community. Rivera believed a literature that captured the memory of an oral folk was the answer in order to discover the different characteristics that shape a particular reality. These aspects include folklore material, such as legends, ballads, jests, superstitions, etc., and the use of Spanish and English to express the bilingual and bicultural reality of the Mexican American people. According to Rivera, an aim of Chicano literature should be to represent the life of its community. See Tomás Rivera, "Into the Labyrinth: The Chicano in Literature," in *The Complete Works of Tomás Rivera* (Houston: Arte Público Press, 1991), 326.

43. A. Paredes, "*With His Pistol in His Hand*," 15.

44. The division of class is expressed in *The Shadow*, a short novel Paredes wrote as a graduate student during the 1950s. *The Shadow* describes the classes of Mexican people (poor vs. rich, Indian vs. Spanish) that lived along the southern side of the Lower Rio Grande Border. The story is set after the Mexican Revolution and explores the problems of a divided society and the issue of a nation in search of itself. See *The Shadow*.

45. A. Paredes, "*With His Pistol in His Hand*," 10.

46. Ibid., 11.

47. Jovita Gonzalez, "America Invades the Border Towns," *Southwest Review* 15 (1930a): 470.

48. J. Gonzalez, "America Invades the Border Towns," 470.

49. John G. Bourke, "The American Congo," *Scribner's Magazine* 15 (1894a): 594.

50. Carey McWilliams, *North from Mexico*, 77.

51. Craig Stinson, "Américo Paredes and the Liberating Potential of Folklore Study," *Folklore Historian* 15 (1998): 34.

52. A. Paredes, "*With His Pistol in His Hand*," 33.

53. James C. Scott, *Weapons of the Weak: Everyday Forms of Peasant Resistance* (New Haven and London: Yale University Press, 1985), xvi.

54. A. Paredes, "*With His Pistol in His Hand*," 37–38.

55. The joke played on the Anglo-Texan begins an investigation by Sheriff W. T (Brack) Morris and one of his deputies, Boone Choate, into a possible horse

theft. Supposedly, the deputy was an expert on the Mexican language, but it was his lack of Spanish fluency that sparked the confrontation between Sheriff Morris and Gregorio Cortez.

56. A. Paredes, "*With His Pistol in His Hand*," 38.

57. Rosa Linda Fregoso, *The Bronze Screen: Chicana and Chicano Film Culture* (Minneapolis and London: University of Minnesota Press, 1993) 73.

58. Victor A. Sorell, "Ethnomusicology, Folklore, and History in the Filmmaker's Art: *The Ballad of Gregorio Cortez*," in *Chicano Cinema: Research, Reviews, and Resources*, ed. Gary D. Keller, 155 (New York: Bilingual Press/Editorial Bilingüe, 1985).

59. Tatcho Mindiola, "El Corrido de Gregorio Cortez," *Southwest Media Review* 3 (Spring 1985): 52–56; Guillermo Hernández, "The Ballad of Gregorio Cortez," *Crítica* 1, no. 3 (Spring 1985): 122–31; Rosa Linda Fregoso, "Zoot Suit and *The Ballad of Gregorio Cortez*," *Crítica* 1:2 (Spring 1985): 126–31; Carl Gutiérrez-Jones, "Legislating Languages: *The Ballad of Gregorio Cortez* and the English Language Amendment," in *Chicanos and Film*, ed. Chon E. Noriega (Minneapolis: University of Minnesota Press, 1992), 195–206.

60. T. Mindiola, "El Corrido de Gregorio Cortez," 53–54.

61. Ibid., 55.

62. A. Paredes, "*With His Pistol in His Hand*," 33.

63. R. L. Fregoso, *The Bronze Screen*, 76–77.

64. Raymund A. Paredes, personal communication, July 8, 2003.

65. Ibid.

66. G. Hernández, "The Ballad of Gregorio Cortez," 123.

Chapter 4

1. Marcus and Fischer, *Anthropology as Cultural Critique*, vii.

2. Edward Burnett Tylor, *Primitive Culture: Researches into the Development of Mythology, Philosophy, Religion, Languages, Art, and Custom*. 2 vols (London: John Murray, 1871), 1:1.

3. William R. Bascom, "Folklore and Anthropology," in *The Study of Folklore*, ed. Alan Dundes, 33 (New Jersey: Prentice-Hall, 1965).

4. Jerry D. Moore, *Visions of Culture: An Introduction to Anthropological Theories and Theorists* (Walnut Creek, Calif.: AltaMira Press, 1997), 128.

5. Alan Barnard, *History and Theory in Anthropology* (Cambridge, UK: Cambridge University Press, 2000), 4–5.

6. Ibid., 5.

7. Franz Boas, "The Limitations of the Comparative Method of Anthropol-

ogy," *Science* n.s. 4 (1896): 901–908, rpt. in *Race, Language, and Culture* (New York: Macmillan, 1940), 273.

8. Ibid., 275.

9. Ibid., 276.

10. Boas, "Race and Progress," *Science* n.s., 74 (1931): 1–8; rpt. in Boas, *Race, Language, and Culture* (New York: Macmillan, 1940), 3–17.

11. Moore, *Visions of Culture*, 51.

12. Marcus and Fischer, *Anthropology as Cultural Critique*, 129–30.

13. Ibid., 131.

14. Virginia Wolf Briscoe, "Ruth Benedict: Anthropological Folklorist," *Journal of American Folklore* 92, no. 366 (October–December 1979): 446.

15. Ibid.

16. Clifford Geertz, *The Interpretation of Cultures* (Basic Books, 1973), 234.

17. Américo Paredes, "Some Aspects of Folk Poetry," *Texas Studies in Literature and Language* 1, no. 6 (1964): 225; see also A. Paredes, *Folklore and Culture*, 127.

18. A. Paredes, "Some Aspects of Folk Poetry," 225.

19. Américo Paredes and George Foss, "The *Décima Cantada* on the Texas-Mexican Border: Four Examples," *Journal of the Folklore Institute* 3 (1966): 91.

20. Américo Paredes, "Folk Medicine and the Intercultural Jest," in *Spanish-Speaking People in the United States*, ed. June Helm, 111, Proceedings of the 1968 Annual Spring Meeting of the American Ethnological Society (Seattle: American Ethnological Society, 1968).

21. Richard Bauman, "Disciplinarity, Reflexivity, and Power in Verbal Art as Performance: A Response," *Journal of American Folklore* 115, no. 455 (Winter 2000): 93.

22. Richard Bauman, introduction to *Toward New Perspectives in Folklore*, ed. Américo Paredes and Richard Bauman, xi (Austin and London: University of Texas Press, 1972).

23. Dan Ben-Amos, "Toward a Definition of Folklore in Context," in Paredes and Bauman, *Toward New Perspectives in Folklore*, 13.

24. Jean François Lyotard, *The Postmodern Condition: A Report on Knowledge*. Trans. Geoff Bennington and Brian Masumo (Minneapolis: University of Minnesota Press, 1984).

25. Alan Barnard, *History and Theory in Anthropology*, 168.

26. James Clifford, "Introduction: Partial Truths," in *Writing Culture: The Poetics and Politics of Ethnography*, ed. James Clifford and George E. Marcus, 11 (Berkeley: University of California Press, 1986).

27. See James Clifford, *The Predicament of Culture: Twentieth-Century*

Ethnography, Literature, and Art (Cambridge: Harvard University Press, 1988); Dennis Tedlock, *The Spoken Word and the Work of Interpretation* (Philadelphia: University of Pennsylvania Press, 1983); Clifford and Marcus, *Writing Culture*.

28. Clifford and Marcus, *Writing Culture*, 18–19.

29. See Clifford, *The Predicament of Culture;* Clifford and Marcus, *Writing Culture;* and Marcus and Fischer, *Anthropology as Cultural Critique*.

30. José E. Limón, "The Return of the Mexican Ballad: Américo Paredes and His Anthropological Text as Persuasive Political Performances," in *Creativity/Anthropology*, ed. Smadar Lavie, Kirin Narayan, and Renato Rosaldo (Ithaca and London: Cornell University Press, 1993), 207.

31. Jerry D. Moore, personal communication, September 2, 2003.

32. Limón, "The Return of the Mexican Ballad," 206.

33. Octavio Romano, "The Anthropology and Sociology of Mexican-Americans: The Distortion of History," *El Grito* 2, no. 1 (1968): 13–26, and "Social Science, Objectivity, and the Chicanos," *El Grito* 4, no. 1 (1970): 4–16; Nick Vaca, "The Mexican-American in the Social Sciences, 1936–1970," *El Grito* 4, no. 1 (1970): 17–51.

34. Renato Rosaldo, " Chicano Studies, 1970–1984," *Annual Review of Anthropology*, 14 (1985): 408; see also Richard R. Flores, in Guerra, *In Memory of Américo Paredes*, 54.

35. Américo Paredes, "On Ethnographic Work among Minority Groups: A Folklorist's Perspective," *New Scholar* 6 (1977): 2; see also A. Paredes, *Folklore and Culture*, 75.

36. Olga Nájera-Ramírez, "Of Fieldwork, Folklore, and Festival: Personal Encounters," *Journal of American Folklore* 444, no. 112 (Spring 1999): 182; Luis Leal, "Américo Paredes and Modern Mexican American Scholarship," *Ethnic Affairs* 1 (Fall 1987): 5.

37. William Hugh Jansen, "The Esoteric-Exoteric Factor in Folklore," in Alan Dundes, *The Study of Folklore* (New Jersey: Prentice-Hall, 1965), 46.

38. R. Bauman, introduction to A. Paredes, *Folklore and Culture*, xxi.

39. Ibid.

40. A. Paredes, "On Ethnographic Work," 29.

41. R. Bauman, introduction to A. Paredes, *Folklore and Culture*, xxi.

42. A. Paredes, "On Ethnographic Work," 22.

43. Ibid., 28.

44. R. Bauman, *Story, Performance, and Event*, 114.

45. Clifford, *The Predicament of Culture;* Tedlock, *The Spoken Word;* Clifford and Marcus, *Writing Culture*.

46. Marcus and Fischer, *Anthropology as Cultural Critique*, vii–xiii.

47. Ibid., viii.

48. Ibid., 36.

49. A. Paredes, "On Ethnographic Work," 11.

50. Marcus and Fischer, *Anthropology as Cultural Critique*, 162.

51. Octavio Paz, *The Labyrinth of Solitude and Other Writings*, trans. Lysander Kemp, Yara Milos, and Rachel Phillips Belash (New York: Grove Press, 1985).

52. Octavio Paz, *México: La última década* (Austin: University of Texas Press, 1969), 10–11.

53. Paz, *The Labyrinth of Solitude*, 82.

54. Américo Paredes, "Estados Unidos, México y el machismo," *Journal of Inter-American Studies* 9, no. 1 (1967): 82; for translation, see "The United States, Mexico, and Machismo," in A. Paredes, *Folklore and Culture*, 232–33.

55. Américo Paredes, "The Problem of Identity in a Changing Culture: Popular Expressions of Culture Conflict along the Lower Rio Grande Border," *Views across the Border: The United States and México*, ed. Stanley Ross, 68–94 (Albuquerque: University of New Mexico Press, 1978).

56. Paz, *The Labyrinth of Solitude*, 16–17.

57. Ibid., 16.

58. Ibid., 15.

59. George J. Sánchez, *Becoming Mexican American: Ethnicity, Culture, and Identity in Chicano Los Angeles, 1900–1945*. (New York: Oxford University Press, 1993).

60. A. Paredes, "The Problem of Identity," 91.

61. O. Paz, *México: La última decáda*, 10–11.

62. A. Paredes, "The Problem of Identity," 92.

63. Calderón and Morín, "Interview," 219.

64. A. Paredes, "The Problem of Identity," 92.

65. A. Paredes, "Acceptance Speech," Aguila Azteca Awards Ceremony, Nov. 20, 1990, typescript, 4, Paredes Papers.

66. John Skirius, *José Vasconcelos y la cruzada de 1929* (México: Siglo Veintiuno Editores, 1978), 52–54, 56.

67. Ibid., 60, 67.

68. Calderón and Morín, "Interview," 219.

69. José Vasconcelos, *La Tormenta: Segunda Parte de Ulises Criollo*, 6th ed. (México: Ediciones Botas, 1937), 302–13.

70. Calderón and Morín, "Interview," 219.

71. A. Paredes, *Uncle Remus con chile* (Houston: Arte Público Press, 1993), 19–20.

72. Ibid., 41.

73. Renato Rosaldo, "Fables of the Fallen Guy," in Calderón and Saldívar, *Criticism in the Borderlands*, 87.

74. Víctor J. Guerra, "*Con Su Pluma en la Mano:* The Legacy of Américo Paredes," in *Hopscotch: A Cultural Review* 2, no. 1 (2000): 86–91.

75. Craig Stinson, "Américo Paredes and the Liberating Potential of Folklore Study," *Folklore Historian* 15 (1998): 31–42.

Conclusion

1. Tish Hinojosa, *Frontejas*, Rounder Records, Cambridge, Mass., 1995.

2. Ibid.

Works of Américo Paredes

1937

Cantos de Adolescencia. San Antonio: Librería Española.

1942

"The Mexico-Texan *Corrido*." *Southwest Review* 27: 470–81.

1947

"Desde Tokio." *El Universal: El Gran Diario de México*, 17 de junio.

1953

"The Love Tragedy in Texas-Mexican Balladry." In *Folk Travelers: Ballads, Tales, and Talk*, ed. Mody C. Boatright, Wilson M. Hudson, and Allen Maxwell, 110–14. Dallas: Southern Methodist University Press.

1957

"The Legend of Gregorio Cortez." In *Mesquite and Willow*, ed. Mody C. Boatright, Wilson M. Hudson, and Allen Maxwell, 3–22. Dallas: Southern Methodist University Press.

1958

"'*El Corrido de José Mosqueda*' as an Example of Pattern in the Ballad." *Western Folklore* 17: 154–62.

"The Mexican *Corrido*: Its Rise and Fall." In *Madstones and Twisters*, ed. Mody C. Boatright, Wilson M. Hudson, and Allen Maxwell, 91–105. Dallas: Southern Methodist University Press.

Review of *American Murder Ballads*, by Olive Wooley Burt. *New Mexico Quarterly* 28: 204–205.

Review of *The Mexican Corrido as a Source for Interpretive Study of Modern Mexico (1870–1950)*, by Merle E. Simmons. *Journal of American Folklore* 71: 582–83.

"With His Pistol in His Hand": A Border Ballad and Its Hero. Austin: University of Texas Press.

1959

"The Bury-Me-Not Theme in the Southwest." In *And Horns on the Toads*, ed. Mody C. Boatright, Wilson M. Hudson, and Allen Maxwell, 88–92. Dallas: Southern Methodist University Press.

Review of *The Restlessness of Shanti Andia and Other Writings*, by Pío Baroja. *Houston Post*, September 13.

"The University of Texas Folklore Archive." *Folklore and Folk Music Archivist* 2, no. 3.

1960

"Gringo." *Western Folklore* 19: 277.

"Luis Inclán: First of the Cowboy Writers." *American Quarterly* 12: 55–70.

"The Mexican Contribution to Our Culture." *Texas Observer*, August 19, 6–7.

"Mexican Riddling Wellerisms." *Western Folklore* 19: 200.

Review of *The True Story of Billy the Kid*, by William Lee Hamlin. *Midwest Folklore* 10: 111–12.

"Tag, You're It." *Journal of American Folklore* 73: 157–58.

"Where Cultures Clashed and Merged." *Texas Observer*, August 12, 7.

1961

"Folklore and History." In *Singers and Storytellers*, ed. Mody C. Boatright, Wilson M. Hudson, and Allen Maxwell, 56–68. Dallas: Southern Methodist University Press.

"Folklore Bibliography for 1960." *Southern Folklore Quarterly* 25: 1–89.

"On *Gringo*, Greaser, and Other Neighborly Names." In *Singers and Storytellers*, ed. Mody C. Boatright, Wilson M. Hudson, and Allen Maxwell, 285–90. Dallas: Southern Methodist University Press.

[Translator.] "Some Forms of the Mexican *Canción*," by Vicente T. Mendoza. In *Singers and Storytellers*, ed. Mody C. Boatright, Wilson M. Hudson, and Allen Maxwell, 46–55. Dallas: Southern Methodist University Press.

[Translator.] "Translations of *Corridos* and *Calaveras*." In *Corridos and Calaveras*, by Edward Larocque Tinker, 41–58. Austin: University of Texas Press.

1962

"*El folklore en los Estados Unidos durante la última década (1953–1962)*." *Folklore Americano* 10: 256–62.

"Folklore Bibliography for 1961." *Southern Folklore Quarterly* 26: 1–96.

Review of *Cantares históricos de la tradición argentina*, ed. Olga Fernández Latour. *Journal of American Folklore* 75: 356.

1963

"The Ancestry of Mexico's *Corridos*: A Matter of Definitions." *Journal of American Folklore* 76: 231–35.

"El cowboy norteamericano en el folklore y la literatura." *Cuadernos del Instituto Nacional de Antropología* 4: 227–40.

"Folklore Bibliography for 1962." *Southern Folklore Quarterly* 27: 1–111.

Review of *Las "pintaderas" mejicanas y sus relaciones*, by José Alcina Franch. *Erasmus* 15: 757–58.

"Texas' Third Man: The Texas-Mexican." *Race: The Journal of the Institute of Race Relations* 4, no. 2: 49–58.

1964

"Folklore Bibliography for 1963." *Southern Folklore Quarterly* 28: 1–94.

"Guitarreros." *Southwest Review* (Autumn).

"La Flora y la Fauna." In *Buying the Wind: Regional Folklore in the United States*, ed. Richard M. Dorson, 454. Chicago: University of Chicago Press.

"Moochers." In *Buying the Wind: Regional Folklore in the United States*, ed. Richard M. Dorson, 453–54. Chicago: University of Chicago Press.

"No Estiendo." In *Buying the Wind: Regional Folklore in the United States*, ed. Richard M. Dorson, 452–53. Chicago: University of Chicago Press.

Review of *Cuentos folklóricos de la Argentina*, by Susana Chertudi. *Journal of American Folklore* 77: 355.

Review of *Treasure of the Sangre de Cristos: Tales and Traditions of the Spanish Southwest*, by Arthur L. Campa. *Journal of American Folklore* 77: 269–70.

"Some Aspects of Folk Poetry." *Texas Studies in Literature and Language* 1, no. 6: 213–25.

[Translator.] *American Extremes*, by Cosío Villegas, Daniel. Austin: University of Texas Press. Originally published as *Extremos de América*. Mexico City: Tesontle, 1949.

[Translator.] "Corrido de Jacinto Treviño." In *Buying the Wind: Regional Folklore in the United States*, ed. Richard M. Dorson, 483–85. Chicago: University of Chicago Press.

[Translator.] "*Pastorela* to Celebrate the Birth of Our Lord Jesus Christ." In *Buying the Wind: Regional Folklore in the United States*, ed. Richard M. Dorson, 466–79. Chicago: University of Chicago Press.

1965

Review of *Cuentos folklóricos de Chile, Vols. 1–3*, by Yolanda Pino Saavedra. *Journal of American Folklore* 78: 171.

Review of *Legends of Texas* and *Happy Hunting Ground*, ed. J. Frank Dobie. *Journal of American Folklore* 78: 163–64.

Review of *Picardía mexicana*, by Armando Jiménez. *Journal of American Folklore* 78: 75–77.

"Vicente T. Mendoza, 1894–1964." *Journal of American Folklore* 78: 154–55.

1966

"The Anglo-American in Mexican Folklore." In *New Voices in American Studies*, ed. Ray B. Browne, Donald M. Winkelman, and Allen Hayman, 113–27. Lafayette, Ind.: Purdue University Studies.

"The *Décima* on the Texas-Mexican Border: Folksong as an Adjunct to Legend." *Journal of the Folklore Institute* 3: 154–67.

"El folklore de los grupos de origen mexicano en Estados Unidos." *Folklore Americano* 14: 146–63.

"El folklore en el XXXVII Congreso Internacional de Americanistas." *Folklore Américas* 26, no. 2: 31–33.

with George Foss. "The *Décima Cantada* on the Texas-Mexican Border: Four Examples." *Journal of the Folklore Institute* 3: 91–115.

1967

"Divergencias en el concepto del folklore y el contexto cultural." *Folklore Américas* 27: 29–38.

"Estados Unidos, México y el machismo." *Journal of Inter-American Studies* 9, no. 1: 65–84.

1968

"Folk Medicine and the Intercultural Jest." In *Spanish-Speaking People in the United States,* ed. June Helm, 104–19. Proceedings of the 1968 Annual Spring Meeting of the American Ethnological Society. Seattle: University of Washington Press.

Review of *Proverbial Comparisons in Ricardo Palma's Tradiciones peruanas,* by Shirley L. Arora. *Romance Philology* 21: 358–59.

"A Selective Annotated Bibliography of Recent Works in Latin American Folklore, 1960–1967." *Handbook of Latin American Studies* 30: 385–410.

"Tributaries to the Mainstream: The Ethnic Groups." In *Our Living Traditions: An Introduction to American Folklore,* ed. Tristram P. Coffin, 70–80. New York: Basic Books.

1969

"Concepts about Folklore in Latin America and the United States." *Journal of the Folklore Institute* 6: 20–38.

1970

Preface in *Bibliografía del folklore chileno (1952–1965),* by Manuel Dannemann Rothstein, vii–viii. Latin American Folklore Series, no. 2, ed. Américo Paredes. Austin: Center for Intercultural Studies in Folklore and Oral History, University of Texas.

Preface in *Las miniaturas en el arte popular mexicano,* by Mauricio Charpenel, vii. Latin American Folklore Series, no. 1, ed. Américo Paredes. Austin: Center for Intercultural Studies in Folklore and Oral History, University of Texas.

"Proverbs and Ethnic Stereotypes." *Proverbium* 15: 95–97.

"The Where and Why of Folklore." *Illinois History* 23, no. 4: 75–76.

[Editor and translator.] *Folktales of Mexico.* Chicago: University of Chicago Press.

1971

"Folklore e historia: Dos cantares de la frontera del norte." In *25 estudios de folklore,* ed. Fernando Anaya Monroy, 209–22. Estudios de Folklore, no. 4. Mexico City: Instituto de Investigaciones Estéticas, Universidad Nacional Autónoma de México.

Foreword in *The Concept of Folklore,* by Paulo de Carvalho Neto, 9–12. Coral Gables, Fla.: University of Miami Press.

"Mexican Legendry and the Rise of the *Mestizo*." In *American Folk Legend: A Symposium*, ed. Wayland D. Hand, 97–107. Berkeley: University of California Press.

Review of *Folk-Lore from the Dominican Republic*, by Manuel J. Andrade, and *Spanish Folk-Tales from New Mexico*, by José Manuel Espinosa. *Hispanic American Historical Review* 51: 556.

Review of *Mexican Tales and Legends from Los Altos*, by Stanley L. Robe. *Hispanic American Historical Review* 51: 544–45.

"The United States, Mexico, and *Machismo*." Trans. Marcy Steen. *Journal of the Folklore Institute* 8: 17–37. Originally published as "Estados Unidos, México y el machismo." *Journal of Inter-American Studies* 9, no. 1 (1967): 65–84.

[Editor] with Ellen J. Stekert. *The Urban Experience and Folk Tradition*. Austin: University of Texas Press.

1972

"Dichos." In *Mexican-American Authors*, ed. Américo Paredes and Raymund Paredes, 27–34. Boston: Houghton Mifflin.

"El concepto de la 'médula emotiva' aplicado al corrido mexicano 'Benjamín Argumedo.'" *Folklore Americano* 17: 139–76.

[Editor] with Raymund Paredes. *Mexican-American Authors*. Boston: Houghton Mifflin.

[Editor] with Richard Bauman. *Toward New Perspectives in Folklore*. Austin: University of Texas Press.

1973

"José Mosqueda and the Folklorization of Actual Events." *Aztlán* 4: 1–30.

Preface in *El Nacimiento del Niño Dios: A Pastorela from Tarimoro, Guanajuato*, by Lily Litvak, vii. Latin American Folklore Series, no. 3, ed. Américo Paredes. Austin: Center for Intercultural Studies in Folklore and Oral History, University of Texas.

1976

"The Role of Folklore in Border Relations." In *San Diego/Tijuana—The International Border in Community Relations: Gateway or Barrier?* ed. Kiki Skagen, 17–22. San Diego: Fronteras.

A Texas-Mexican Cancionero: Folksongs of the Lower Border. Urbana: University of Illinois Press.

1977

"Jorge Isidoro Sánchez y Sánchez (1906–1972)." In *Humanidad: Essays in Honor of George I. Sánchez*, ed. Américo Paredes, 120–26. Los Angeles: Chicano Studies Research Center Publications, University of California.

"On Ethnographic Work among Minority Groups: A Folklorist's Perspective." *New Scholar* 6: 1–32.

"Yamashita, Zapata, and the Arthurian Legend." *Western Folklore* 36: 160–63.

[Editor.] *Humanidad: Essays in Honor of George I. Sánchez*. Los Angeles: Chicano Studies Research Center Publications, University of California.

1978

"'El romance de la Isla de Jauja' en el suroeste de Estados Unidos." *Logos: Revista de la Facultad de Filosofía y Letras de la Universidad de Buenos Aires* 13–14: 399–406.

"The Problem of Identity in a Changing Culture: Popular Expressions of Culture Conflict along the Lower Rio Grande Border." In *Views across the Border: The United States and Mexico*, ed. Stanley Ross, 68–94. Albuquerque: University of New Mexico Press.

1979

"The Folk Base of Chicano Literature." In *Modern Chicano Writers: A Collection of Critical Essays*, ed. Joseph Sommers and Tomás Ybarra-Frausto; trans. Kathleen Lamb, 4–17. Englewood Cliffs, N.J.: Prentice-Hall. Originally published as "El folklore de los grupos de origen mexicano en Estados Unidos." *Folklore Americano* 14 (1966): 146–63.

1982

"Folklore, *Lo Mexicano*, and Proverbs." *Aztlán* 13: 1–11.

1983

"The *Corrido:* Yesterday and Today." In *Ecology and Development of the Border Region*, ed. Stanley R. Ross, 293–97. Mexico City: Asociación Nacional de Universidades e Institutos de Enseñanza Superior.

"Nearby Places and Strange-Sounding Names." In *The Texas Literary Tradition: Fiction, Folklore, History*, ed. Don Graham, James W. Lee, and William T.

Pilkington, 130–38. Austin: University of Texas and Texas State Historical Association.

1987

"The Undying Love of '*El Indio*' Córdova: *Décimas* and Oral History in a Border Family." *Ernesto Galarza Commemorative Lecture: Inaugural Lecture, 1986*. Stanford: Stanford Center for Chicano Research, Stanford University.

1990

George Washington Gómez: A Mexicotexan Novel. Houston: Arte Público Press.

"Acceptance Speech." Aguila Azteca Awards Ceremony, November 20. Typescript. Américo Paredes Papers. Benson Latin American Collection, General Libraries, University of Texas at Austin.

1991

Between Two Worlds. Houston: Arte Público Press.

1993

Folklore and Culture on the Texas-Mexican Border. Ed. Richard Bauman. Austin: Center for Mexican American Studies, University of Texas at Austin.

Uncle Remus con chile. Houston: Arte Público Press.

1994

The Hammon and the Beans and Other Stories. Houston: Arte Público Press.

1998

"Mi Tía Pilar." *Reflexiones: New Directions in Mexican American Studies*. Austin: Center for Mexican American Studies.

The Shadow. Houston: Arte Público Press.

1999

"Mr. White." *Reflexiones: New Directions in Mexican American Studies*. Austin: Center for Mexican American Studies.

Bibliography

Alessio Robles, Vito. *Monterrey en la historia y en la leyenda*. Mexico City: Antigua Librería Robredo de José Porrúa e Hijos, 1936.

Anzaldúa, Gloria. *Borderlands/La Frontera: The New Mestiza*. San Francisco: Spinsters/Aunt Lute, 1987.

Aristotle. *Poetics*. Trans. with an introduction and notes by Gerald F. Else. Ann Arbor: University of Michigan Press, 1970.

Arreola, Daniel D. *Tejano South Texas: A Mexican American Cultural Province*. Austin: University of Texas Press, 2002.

Bancroft, Hubert Howe. *The Works*. Vol. 18. San Francisco: A. L. Bancroft, 1884.

Barnard, Alan. *History and Theory in Anthropology*. Cambridge, UK: Cambridge University Press, 2000.

Bartlett, John Russell. *Personal Narrative of Explorations and Incidents in Texas, New Mexico, California, Sonora, and Chihuahua Connected with the United States and Mexican Boundary Commission during the Years 1850, '51, '52, and '53*. 1854. Rpt. Chicago: Rio Grande Press, 1965.

Bascom, William R. "Folklore and Anthropology." In *The Study of Folklore*, ed. Alan Dundes. New Jersey: Prentice-Hall, 1965.

Bauman, Richard. "Disciplinarity, Reflexivity, and Power in Verbal Art as Performance: A Response," *Journal of American Folklore* 115, no. 455 (Winter 2000).

———. Introduction to *Folklore and Culture on the Texas-Mexican Border*, by Américo Paredes ix–xxiii. Austin: Center for Mexican American Studies and University of Texas Press, 1993.

———. Introduction to *Toward New Perspectives in Folklore*, ed. Richard Bauman and Américo Paredes, xi–xv. Austin: University of Texas Press, 1972.

———. *Story, Performance, and Event: Contextual Studies of Oral Narrative*. New York: Cambridge University Press, 1986.

Bauman, Richard, and Roger D. Abrahams, eds. *"And Other Neighborly Names": Social Process and Cultural Image in Texas Folklore*. Austin and London: University of Texas Press, 1981.

Ben-Amos, Dan. "Toward a Definition of Folklore in Context." In *Toward New Perspectives in Folklore*, ed. Richard Bauman and Américo Paredes, 3–15. Austin: University of Texas Press, 1972.

Bhabha, Homi K. *The Location of Culture*. London and New York: Routledge, 1994.

Bloom, Harold. *The Anxiety of Influence: A Theory of Poetry*. New York: Oxford University Press, 1973.

Boas, Franz. "The Limitations of the Comparative Method of Anthropology." *Science*, n.s. 4 (1896): 901–908. Rpt. in *Race, Language, and Culture*, 270–80. New York: Macmillan, 1940.

———. "Race and Progress," *Science* n.s., 74 (1931): 1–8. Rpt. in Boas, *Race, Language, and Culture*, 3–17. New York: Macmillan, 1940.

Boatright, Mody C. Papers. Center for American History, Archives and Manuscripts, University of Texas at Austin.

Bourke, John G. "The American Congo," *Scribner's Magazine* 15 (1894a): 590–610.

Briscoe, Virginia Wolf. "Ruth Benedict: Anthropological Folklorist." *Journal of American Folklore* 92, no. 366 (October–December 1979): 446.

Bruce-Novoa, Juan. *Chicano Authors: Inquiry by Interview*. Austin: University of Texas Press, 1980.

Brunvard, Jan Harold. *The Study of American Folklore: An Introduction*. New York: W. W. Norton, 1968.

Cabeza de Vaca, Fabiola. *We Fed Them Cactus*. Albuquerque: University of New Mexico Press, 1954.

Calderón, Héctor. "Literatura fronteriza tejana: El compromiso con la historia en Américo Paredes, Rolando Hinojosa y Gloria Anzaldúa." *Mester: Literary Journal of the Graduate Students of the Department of Spanish and Portuguese University of California* 12, 13, no. 2–1 (Fall–Spring 1993–94): 41–61.

———. "Reinventing the Border." In *American Mosaic: Multicultural Readings in Context*, ed. Barbara Roche Rico and Sandra Mano. Boston: Houghton Mifflin, 1995.

———. "Texas Border Literature: Cultural Transformation and Historical Reflection in the Works of Américo Paredes, Rolando Hinojosa, and Gloria Anzaldúa." *Dispositio* 16, no. 41 (1991–92).

Calderón, Héctor, and José Morín. "Interview with Américo Paredes." *Nepantla: Views from South* 1, no. 1 (2000): 197–228.

Calderón, Héctor, and José David Saldívar, eds. *Criticism in the Borderlands: Studies in Chicano Literature, Culture, and Ideology*. Durham and London: Duke University Press, 1991.

Campa, Arthur L. *Arthur L. Campa and the Coronado Cuarto Centennial*. Ed. Anselmo F. Arellano and Julian Josue Vigil. Las Vegas, N.Mex.: Editorial Telerana, 1980.

———. "Cultural Variations in the Anglo-Spanish Southwest." *Western Review* 7 (Spring 1970).

———. *Hispanic Culture in the Southwest*. Oklahoma: University of Oklahoma Press, 1979.

———. "Juan de Oñate Was Mexican: The Coronado Cuarto Centennial and the Spaniards." In *Arthur L. Campa and the Coronado Cuarto Centennial*, ed. Anselmo F. Arellano and Julian Josue Vigil. Las Vegas, N.Mex.: Editorial Telerana, 1980.

———. *Spanish Folk-Poetry in New Mexico*. Albuquerque: University of New Mexico Press, 1946.

———. "The Spanish Folksong in the Southwest." *University of New Mexico Bulletin, Modern Language Series* 1, no. 4 (1933).

Cantú, Norma E., and Olga Nájera-Ramírez, eds. *Chicana Traditions: Continuity and Change*. Urbana: University of Illinois Press, 2002.

Cisneros, Sandra. *The House on Mango Street*. Houston: Arte Público Press,1986.

Clifford, James. *The Predicament of Culture: Twentieth-Century Ethnography, Literature, and Art*. Cambridge: Harvard University Press, 1988.

Clifford, James, and George E. Marcus, eds. *Writing Culture: The Poetics and Politics of Ethnography*. Berkeley: University of California Press, 1986.

Cohn, Martin A. *The Martyr: The Story of a Secret Jew and the Mexican Inquisition in the Sixteenth Century*. Philadelphia: Jewish Publication Society of America, 1973.

Cox, I. J. "The Southwest Boundary of Texas." *Southwest Historical Quarterly* 1, no. 2 (October 1902): 81–102.

Cumberland, Charles C. "Border Raids in the Lower Rio Grande Valley—1915." *Southwestern Historical Quarterly* 57, No. 3. (January 1954): 285–311.

Dobie, J. Frank, ed. *Publications of the Texas Folk-Lore Society*. Vol. 4. Austin: Texas Folklore Society, 1925.

———. *Puro Mexicano*. Dallas: Southern Methodist University Press, 1935.

Dorson, Richard M. *American Folklore*. Chicago: University of Chicago Press, 1959.

Dundes, Alan. "The American Concept of Folklore." *Journal of the Folklore Institute* 3 (1966): 226–49.

Espinosa, Aurelio M. *Cuentos populares españoles*. 3 vols. Stanford: Stanford University Press, 1923–26.

———. *The Folklore of Spain in the American Southwest: Traditional Spanish Folk Literature in Northern New Mexico and Southern Colorado*, ed. J. Manuel Espinosa, 50–64. Norman: University of Oklahoma Press, 1985.

———. "New Mexican Spanish Folklore: Part 1, Myths; Part 2, Superstitions and Beliefs." *Journal of American Folklore* 23 (1910): 395–418.

———. "New Mexican Spanish Folklore: Part 3, Folktales." *Journal of American Folklore* 24 (1911): 397–444.

Espinosa, J. Manuel. "Major Stages in the Development of Espinosa's Folklore Studies." In Aurelio M. Espinosa, *The Folklore of Spain in the American Southwest*, ed. J. Manuel Espinosa. Norman and London: University of Oklahoma Press, 1985.

Ferehnbach, T. R. *Lone Star: A History of Texas and the Texans*. New York: Macmillan, 1968.

Fischer, Michael M. J. "Ethnicity and the Post-Modern Arts of Memory." In *Writing Culture: The Poetics and Politics of Ethnography: A School of Research Advanced Seminar*, ed. James Clifford and George E. Marcus, 194–233. Berkeley: University of California Press,1986.

Forto, Emilio C. "Actual Situation on the River Rio Grande." *Pan American Labor Press*, September 11, 1918.

Freeman, Derek. *Margaret Mead and Samoa: The Making and Unmaking of an Anthropological Myth*. Cambridge: Harvard University Press, 1983.

Fregoso, Rosa Linda. *The Bronze Screen: Chicana and Chicano Film Culture*. Minneapolis and London: University of Minnesota Press, 1993.

———. "Zoot Suit and the Ballad of Gregorio Cortez." *Crítica* 1, no. 2 (Spring 1985): 126–31.

Galarza, Ernesto. *Barrio Boy*. New York: Ballantine Books, 1972.

García, Kimberly. "Author Battles Racist Views." *Brownsville Herald*, August 4, 1991.

Garza-Falcón, Leticia Magda. *Gente Decente: A Borderlands Response to the Rhetoric of Dominance*. Austin: University of Texas Press, 1998.

Geertz, Clifford. *The Interpretation of Cultures*. Basic Books, 1973.

Goldfinch, Charles W. *The Mexican American*. New York: Arno Press, 1974.

Gómez-Quiñones, Juan, José Limón, Teresa McKenna, and Victor Nelson. Interview with Américo Paredes, August 23, 1984, Austin, Tex. Copy in author's possession.

González, Jovita. "America Invades the Border Towns." *Southwest Review* 15 (1930): 469–77.

———. "Social Life in Cameron, Starr, and Zapata Counties." Master's thesis, University of Texas, 1930.

———. "Tales and Songs of the Texas-Mexicans." In *Man, Bird, and Beast*, 86–116. Austin: Texas Folk-Lore Society, 1930.

González, Roberto C. "A Hero and a Mentor: Américo Paredes's Legacy Lives on in His Works." *Brownsville Herald*, May 19, 1999.

Griswold del Castillo, Richard. *The Treaty of Guadalupe Hidalgo: A Legacy of Conflict*. Norman and London: University of Oklahoma Press, 1990.

Guerra, Víctor J. "Con Su Pluma en La Mano: The Legacy of Américo Paredes." *Hopscotch: A Cultural Review* 2, no.1 (2000): 86–91.

———, ed. *In Memory of Américo Paredes*. Center for Mexican American Studies, University of Texas at Austin, May 23, 1999.

Guevara-Vásquez, Rey. "Maverick Scholar Fighting to Correct History's Prejudice." *Austin-American Statesman*, February 7, 1982.

Gutiérrez-Jones, Carl. "Legislating Languages: The Ballad of Gregorio Cortez and the English Language Amendment." In *Chicanos and Film*, ed. Chon E. Noriega, 195–206. Minneapolis: University of Minnesota Press, 1992.

Hernández, Guillermo. "The Ballad of Gregorio Cortez." *Crítica* 1, no. 3 (Spring 1985): 122–31.

Hernández, José. *Martín Fierro*. Buenos Aires: Editorial Universitaria, 1961.

Herrera-Sobek, María. "Américo Paredes: A Tribute." *Mexican Studies/Estudios Mexicanos* 16, no. 2 (2000).

Hill, Lawrence Francis. *José de Escandón and the Founding of Nuevo Santander: A Study in Spanish Colonization*. Columbus: Ohio State University Press, 1926.

Hinojosa, Tish. *Frontejas*. Rounder Records. Cambridge, Mass., 1995.

Hinojosa-Smith, Rolando. Introduction to *George Washington Gómez: A Mexicotexan Novel,* by Américo Paredes. Houston: Arte Público Press, 1990.

———. "This Writer's Sense of Place." In *The Texas Literary Tradition: Fiction, Folklore, History*, ed. Don Graham et al., 120–24. Austin: College of Liberal Arts, University of Texas at Austin, Texas State Historical Association, 1983.

Holley, Joe. "With His Guitar in His Hand." *Texas Observer*, October 29, 1993.

Holley, Mary Austin. *Texas: Observations, Historical, Geographical, and Descriptive*. Rpt. Austin, 1935.

Jameson, Fredric. *The Political Unconscious: Narrative as a Socially Symbolic Act*. New York: Cornell University Press, 1981.

Jansen, William Hugh. "The Esoteric-Exoteric Factor in Folklore." *Fabula: Journal of Folktale Studies* 2 (1959): 205–11.

Jaramillo, Cleofas M. *Shadows of the Past (Sombras del Pasado)*. Santa Fe: Seton Village Press, 1941.

Johnson, Benjamin Heber. *Revolution in Texas: How a Forgotten Rebellion and Its Bloody Suppression Turned Mexicans into Americans*. New Haven and London: Yale University Press, 2003.

Lavie, Smadar, Kirin Narayan, and Renato Rosaldo, eds. *Creativity/Anthropology*. Ithaca and London: Cornell University Press, 1993.

Leach, Mary. *The Standard Dictionary of Folklore, Mythology, and Legend*. 2 vols. New York: Funk and Wagnalls, 1949–50.

Leal, Luis. "Américo Paredes and Modern Mexican American Scholarship." *Ethnic Affairs* 1 (Fall 1987).

León, Alonso de. *Historia de Nuevo León*. Ed. Israel Cavazos Garza. Monterrey: Gobierno del Estado de Nuevo León, 1961.

Liebman, Seymour B. *The Jews in New Spain: Faith, Flame, and the Inquisition*. Coral Gables, Fla.: University of Miami Press, 1970.

Limón, José E. "Américo Paredes: A Man from the Border." *Revista Chicano-Riqueña* 8, no. 3 (1980).

———. *Dancing with the Devil: Society and Cultural Poetics in Mexican-American South Texas*. Madison: University of Wisconsin Press, 1994.

———. *Mexican Ballads, Chicano Poems: History and Influence in Mexican-American Social Poetry*. Berkeley: University of California Press, 1992.

———. "The Return of the Mexican Ballad: Américo Paredes and His Anthropological Text as Persuasive Political Performance." In *Creativity/Anthropology*, ed. Smadar Lavie, Kirin Narayan, and Renato Rosaldo, 184–210. Ithaca and London: Cornell University Press, 1993.

López de Santa Anna, Antonio. "Manifesto Relative to His Operations in the Texas Campaign and His Capture." *The Mexican Side of the Texas Revolution*, trans. and notes Carlos E. Castañeda. Austin: Graphic Ideas, 1970.

Lummis, Charles F. *The Land of Poco Tiempo*. New York: Charles Scribner's Sons, 1893.

———. *The Spanish Pioneers*. Chicago: Charles McClurg, 1893.

Lyotard, Jean François. *The Postmodern Condition: A Report on Knowledge*. Trans. Geoff Bennington and Brian Masumo. Minneapolis: University of Minnesota Press, 1984.

Madsen, William. *The Mexican American in South Texas*. New York: Holt, Rinehart and Winston, 1964.

Marcus, George E., and Michael M. J. Fischer. *Anthropology as Cultural Critique: An Experimental Moment in the Human Sciences*. Chicago: University of Chicago Press, 1986.

McDowell, John Holmes. "The *Corrido* of Greater Mexico as Discourse, Music, and Event." In *"And Other Neighborly Names": Social Process and Cultural Image in Texas Folklore*, ed. Roger D. Abrahams and Richard Bauman, 44–75. Austin and London: University of Texas Press, 1981.

McNutt, James Charles. "Beyond Regionalism: Texas Folklorists and the Emergence of a Post-Regional Consciousness." Ph. D. diss., University of Texas at Austin, 1982.

McWilliams, Carey. *North of Mexico: The Spanish-Speaking People of the United States*. New York: Praeger, 1990.

Mindiola, Tatcho. "El Corrido de Gregorio Cortez." *Southwest Media Review* 3 (Spring 1985): 52–56.

Montejano, David. *Anglos and Mexicans in the Making of Texas, 1836–1986*. Austin: University of Texas Press, 1987.

Moore, Jerry D. *Visions of Culture: An Introduction to Anthropological Theories and Theorists*. Walnut Creek, Calif.: AltaMira Press, 1997.

Nájera-Ramírez, Olga. "Of Fieldwork, Folklore, and Festival: Personal Encounters." *Journal of American Folklore*, 112 (Spring 1999): 444.

Newell, William Wells. "The Study of Folklore." *Transactions of the New York Academy of Sciences* 9 (1890).

Oring, Elliott. "Folk Narratives." In *Folk Groups and Folklore Genres: An Introduction*, ed. Elliott Oring, 121–45. Logan: Utah State University Press, 1986.

Otero-Warren, Nina. *Old Spain in Our Southwest*. New York: Harcourt, Brace, 1936.

Paredes, Américo. Papers. 1886–1999. Benson Latin American Collection, General Libraries, University of Texas at Austin.

Paredes, Raymund A. "The Evolution of Chicano Literature." In *Three American Literatures: Essay in Chicano, Native American, and Asian American Literature for Teachers of American Literature*, ed. Houston A. Baker. New York: Modern Language Association of America, 1982.

———. "The Mexican Image in American Travel Literature, 1831–1869." *New Mexico Historical Review* (1977): 5–29.

———. "The Origins of Anti-Mexican Sentiment in the United States." In *New Directions in Chicano Scholarship*, ed. Ricardo Romo and Raymund Paredes, 139–65. San Diego: Regents of the University of California, 1978.

Paz, Octavio. *El Laberinto de la Soledad*. México : Cuadernos Americanos, 1950. Rev. ed. México: FCE, 1959.

———. *The Labyrinth of Solitude and Other Writings*. Trans. Lysander Kemp, Yara Milos, and Rachel Phillips Belash. New York: Grove Press, 1985.

———. *México: La última década*. Austin: University of Texas Press, 1969.

Peña, Manuel, and Richard Bauman. "Américo Paredes (1915–1999)." *Journal of American Folklore* 113 (Spring 2000): 195–98.

Pérez de Villagrá, Gaspar. *History of New Mexico*. Trans. and ed. Gilberto Espinosa. Los Angeles: Quivara Society, 1933.

Pérez-Torres, Rafael. *Movements in Chicano Poetry: Against Myths, against Margins*. New York: Cambridge University Press, 1995.

Pierce, Frank C. *A Brief History of the Lower Rio Grande Valley*. Menasha, Wisc.: George Banta Publishing, 1917.

Pike, Zebulon M. *The Expeditions of Zebulon Montgomery Pike to Headwaters of the Mississippi River, through Louisiana Territory, and in New Spain, during the Years 1805–6–7*. Vol. 2. Ed. Elliot Coues. New York: Frances P. Harper, 1895.

Porterfield, Billy. "Twilight of a Great Man: Illness Makes Work Harder for Hispanic UT Scholar, 74." *Austin-American Statesman*, July, 28, 1989.

Prieto, Alejandro. *Historia, Geografía, y Estadística del Estado de Tamaulipas*. Mexico, 1873. Reproducción Facsimilar de la Edición de 1873. S.A. Librería, México, D.F.: Manuel Porrúa, 1949.

Reyna, José R. *Raza Humor: Chicano Joke Tradition in Texas*. San Antonio, Tex.: Penca Books, 1980.

Rivera, Tomás. "Into the Labyrinth: The Chicano in Literature." In *The Complete Works of Tomás Rivera*, 325–37. Houston: Arte Público Press, 1991.

Robinson, Cecil. *With the Ears of Strangers: The Mexican in American Literature*. Tucson: University of Arizona Press, 1963.

Romano, Octavio Ignacio. "The Anthropology and Sociology of Mexican-Americans: The Distortion of History." *El Grito* 2, no. 1 (1968): 13–26.

———. "Social Science, Objectivity, and the Chicanos." *El Grito* 4, no. 1 (1970): 4–16.

Rosaldo, Renato. "Chicano Studies, 1970–1984." *Annual Review of Anthropology* 14 (1985): 405–21.

———. *Culture and Truth: The Remaking of Social Analysis*. Boston: Beacon Press, 1993.

———. "Fables of the Fallen Guy." In *Criticism in the Borderlands: Studies in Chicano Literature, Culture, and Ideology*, ed. Héctor Calderón and José David Saldívar, 84–93. Durham and London: Duke University Press, 1991.

Said, Edward W. *Orientalism*. New York: Random House, 1979.

———. *Representations of the Intellectual*. New York: Random House, 1994.

Saldívar, José David. "Chicano Border Narratives as Cultural Critique." In *Criticism in the Borderlands: Studies in Chicano Literature, Culture, and Ideology*, ed. Héctor Calderón and José David Saldívar, 167–80. Durham and London: Duke University Press, 1991.

Saldívar, Ramón. *Chicano Narrative: The Dialects of Difference*. Madison: University of Wisconsin Press, 1990.

———. Introduction to *The Hammon and the Beans and Other Stories*, by Américo Paredes, vii–li. Houston: Arte Público Press, 1994.

Sánchez, George J. *Becoming Mexican American: Ethnicity, Culture, and Identity in Chicano Los Angeles, 1900–1945*. New York: Oxford University Press, 1993.

Sandos, James. *Rebellion in the Borderlands: Anarchism and the Plan of San Diego, 1904–1923*. Norman and London: University of Oklahoma Press, 1992.

Santa María, Vicente de. *Relación Histórica de la Colonia del Nuevo Santander*. México: Universidad Nacional Autónoma de México Dirección General de Publicaciones, 1973.

Scott, James C. *Weapons of the Weak: Everyday Forms of Peasant Resistance*. New Haven and London: Yale University Press, 1985.

Scott, Winfield. *Memoirs*. 2 vols. New York: Sheldon Publishers, 1864.

Shakespeare, William. *The Merchant of Venice*. *The Globe Illustrated Shakespeare: The Complete Works Annotated*. Ed. Howard Staunton. New York: Gramercy Books, 1979.

Simmons, Merle. *The Mexican Corrido as a Source for Interpretive Study of Mexico (1870–1950)*. Bloomington: Indiana University Press, 1957.

Skirius, John. *José Vasconcelos y la cruzada de 1929*. México: Siglo Veintiuno Editores, 1978.

———. "Octavio Paz [1914–]." In *El Ensayo Hispano-Americano del Siglo XX*, 406–49. 3rd ed. Comp. John Skirius. México: Fondo de Cultura Económica, 1994.

Smithwick, Noah. *The Evolution of a State; Or, Recollections of Old Texas Days*. 1900. Rpt. Austin: Steck-Vaughn, 1986.

Sorell, Victor A. "Ethnomusicology, Folklore, and History in the Filmmaker's Art: The Ballad of Gregorio Cortez." In *Chicano Cinema: Research, Reviews, and Resources*, ed. Gary D. Keller, 153–58. New York: Bilingual Press/Editorial Bilingüe, 1985.

Spell, L. "The First Teacher of European Music in North America." *Catholic Historical Quarterly* n.s. 2 (October 1922).

Stilwell, Hart. *Border City*. New York: Doubleday and Doran, 1945.

Stinson, Craig. "Américo Paredes and the Liberating Potential of Folklore Study." *Folklore Historian* 15 (1998): 31–42.

Tedlock, Dennis. *The Spoken Word and the Work of Interpretation*. Philadelphia: University of Pennsylvania Press, 1983.

Tylor, Edward Burnett. *Primitive Culture: Researches into the Development of Mythology, Philosophy, Religion, Languages, Art, and Custom*. 2 vols. London: John Murray, 1871.

Vaca, Nick. "The Mexican-American in the Social Sciences, 1936–1970." *El Grito* 4, no. 1 (1970): 17–51.

Vasconcelos, José. *La raza cósmica—misión de la raza iberoamericana—notas de viajes a la Américoa del sur*. París: Agencia Mundial de Librería, 1925.

———. *La Tormenta: Segunda Parte de "Ulises Criollo*." 6th ed. México: Ediciones Botas, 1937.

Webb, Walter Prescott. *The Texas Rangers: A Century of Frontier Defense*. Boston and New York: Houghton Mifflin, 1935. Rpt., Austin: University of Texas Press, 1965.

West, John O., comp. and ed. *Mexican-American Folklore: Legends, Songs, Festivals, Proverbs, Crafts, Tales of Saints, of Revolutions, and More*. Little Rock: August House, 1989.

Index

Abrahams, Roger D., 63–64, 82, 103, 106
Adams, Rick, 63
American Folklore Society, 22, 67, 130; Journal of, 102, 106
Anglo and North American, 12, 14–23, 32–34, 73, 90, 92–94, 98, 113–14, 120–21, 123–24, 128; attitudes toward Mexican and Indian, 10–12, 14–15, 20, 24, 47–48, 62, 70, 74–75, 84–85, 88–89, 92, 110, 127; attitudes toward Mexican women, 16; complex, superiority, of, 10–12, 14, 20–21, 24, 47, 63, 76–77, 88; as immigrants, 3, 11–13, 72; as gringos, 17, 39–40, 70, 91; as Midwesterner, 17; as outsiders, 25, 97, 117; as Texan, 1, 11–13, 22, 24, 47, 79, 90–91, 94–95, 121, 124–25; women, 124
anthropology, American, 56, 63–64, 71, 83, 85, 90, 92, 103, 105–106, 120, 128; branches of, 98; classic period of, 97–102, 107–108, 111; concept of, 98, 99, 100–102; postmodern period of, 97–98, 107–18, 123–26; relationship with folklore, 71, 85, 90, 92, 97–99, 101–102, 105–18, 125–26, 128

Bauman, Richard, 64, 82, 103, 106
Benedict, Ruth, 101–102
Boas, Franz, 99–101
Boatright, Mody C., 63–64, 79
Brownsville Herald, 47, 54, 56
Brownsville Junior College, 43, 47

Calderón, Héctor, 71, 83, 86–87
Campa, Arthur L., 25, 28–31
Cantos de Adolescencia, 43–47
Carvajal, Luis de, y de la Cueva, 4–6, 8
Center for Mexican American Studies, 64–66, 68; Américo Paredes Center for Cultural Studies, 130; books, 131; Intercultural Studies in Folklore and Ethnomusicology, 130; Intercultural Studies in Folklore and Oral Tradition, 64, 66
China, 56, 58
citizenship, U.S., 59; Mexican, 13
Clifford, James, 109
Cortez, Gregorio, 35, 71, 73–75, 83, 85, 92–96; Corrido of, 3–4, 34, 60–61, 71, 75–77, 79–80
Cortez, Román, 70, 74, 80, 83, 90–94
Cortina, Juan N., 15, 31, 34
cowboy, Texas. See Mexican vaquero

Daily Texan, 65
Dallas Times Herald, 59
Dobie, J. Frank, 22–24, 30–31, 47–48, 73, 79, 110, 128

Escandón, José de, 7–9, 11, 72
Espinosa, Aurelio M., 25–28, 31, 79
Ethnographic Work, On, 97, 110–18

Fischer, Michael M. J., 109, 115–18
folklore as oral tradition, 2–3, 9–11, 14, 19, 22, 34–35, 42, 70–71, 73, 78; concept of, 1–3, 21–32, 49, 60, 63–64, 66, 73, 75, 77–78, 81, 89–90, 92–94, 103, 106–14, 117, 125–28; items of, 1, 22–23, 25, 31, 34–35, 41–42, 50, 53, 60, 70–71, 73, 75–81, 90–91, 104–105, 125; methods and approaches of, 2–3, 22–23, 25–31, 75, 77–78, 128; as performance, 2–3, 24–25, 42, 49–54, 64, 72–73, 75, 80, 83, 89–94, 97–99, 103–14, 117, 123–28; relationship with anthropology, 71, 85, 90, 92, 97–99, 101–102, 105–18, 125–26, 128
Frankel, Charles, award, 67, 130

George Washington Gómez, 47–49, 52, 130
González, Jovita, 16, 25, 30–31, 88
Great Depression, the, 43, 47

Hinojosa, Tish, 82, 131–32
Hinojosa-Smith, Rolando, 9, 82–84

Indian, 3, 5–12, 14, 19, 21, 87–88, 116, 118; Apache, 87; attacks, 6–8, 12, 87; Aztec, 121; chichimecas, 7; Comanche, 21, 87; English policy toward, 11; rancherías, 9; Spanish policy toward, 9–11, 72, 118

Jansen, William H., 112, 123
Japan, 56, 58; officials, 56; people, 19, 58; Tokyo, 57–58
Jewish people, 2, 4–6, 37, 100, 124

Korea, 56, 58; War, 102, 124

Limón, José E., 68, 71, 83–85, 87
Lomax, John A., 22, 79

McWilliams, Carey, 88
Malinowski, Bronislaw, 99
Marcus, George E., 109, 115–18
Mendoza, Vicente, 60, 77–78, 119
Mexican, 1–4, 9, 14–15, 17–21, 23–24, 26, 28–32, 39, 43, 47–50, 55–56, 73–74, 78, 88, 90–96, 105–106, 110, 114, 118–24, 127–30; as American, 3, 21, 25, 27, 29, 31–32, 43, 48–49, 52–54, 78, 85–87, 97, 103, 105–106, 108–109, 111, 114, 118–30; attitudes toward Anglo American, 70, 77, 90–92, 94, 97–98, 105, 111–12, 125, 128; as border, 10, 18–19, 25, 34, 36–37, 49–52, 54, 72–73, 87, 110, 117, 124; as Chicano(a), 3, 38–39, 45, 64–66, 71, 78, 81–87, 109–10, 112–13, 118, 120, 122, 128; genius of, 3, 10, 23–25, 32, 49–54, 83, 89–92, 97, 104–105, 108, 111–14, 117; as macho, 95, 102, 119–20, 124; middle-class, 85, 88–89, 130; as nationals, 118–23; negative stereotypes of, 12, 14–16, 19, 20–22, 24–25, 48–49, 53, 75, 88–92, 94–96, 98, 103, 110, 113–14, 117, 119, 120–28; as Spanish, 26–29, 54, 78–79, 114; as Tejano, 4, 14, 18, 23, 30, 37, 39–41, 43–44, 48, 70, 73, 76, 78–79, 82, 88, 92–93, 103, 106, 108–109, 112, 116–17, 124–25, 127–28; vaquero, 14, 16, 18, 22, 31, 70, 92, 95; women, 16, 124

Monroe Doctrine, the, 35
Montelongo, Ignacio, 36

New Perspectives in Folklore, Towards, 106
Nuevo Reino de León, 4–6
Nuevo Santander, 3–4, 8–10, 71–72

Order of Aztec Eagle, award 67, 123; speech, 130–31

Pacific Stars and Stripes, 56, 58
Paredes, Raymund A., 78, 82
Paredes family members: Justo 2, 34–37; Clotilde Manzano, 33; Eliseo, 34; Eleazar, 56; Amador, 56, 67; Alan, 59, 131; Amador, 56, 67; Amelia Shidzu, 58–59, 62, 131; Américo Jr., 55, 131; Julie, 62, 131; Vicente, 62, 131
Paz, Octavio, 118–21, 128

Ramos, Samuel, 119
Reyna, José R., 111–12
Rivera, Tomás, 82–84
Romano, Octavio I., 110
Rosaldo, Renato, 71, 83, 85, 87, 125

Saldívar, José David, 71, 83–83
Saldívar, Ramón, 71, 83, 86
Santa Anna, Antonio López de, 13–14
Shadow, The, 59
Silva, Consuelo, 55
Simmons, Merle E., 41
Spain, 2, 4–7, 25–28, 75; New Spain, 5–9, 16, 35, 72, 79; Spaniards, 4–10, 26, 29, 54, 78–79, 114
Stephenson, Robert, 60
Stilwell, Hart, 54

Terry, Francis, 68
Texas Folklore Society, 22, 31, 63–64, 106–107
Texas Rangers, 2, 14, 19, 23, 35, 52, 61–62, 69, 74, 76–78, 84, 95, 124, 131
Thompson, Stith, 60–61

Uncle Remus con chile, 123–25
United States Expansionism, 2, 10–21, 32, 34–36, 72, 73, 89, 95, 97, 102–103, 127, 129–30; as hegemony, 97, 102–103, 107, 130; as Manifest Destiny, 11, 14, 73
University of Texas at Austin (UT), 4, 59–61, 63–68, 103, 106, 121, 130–31
University of Texas Press, 61–62

Vaca, Nick, 110
Vasconcelos, José, 122, 128
Vespucci, Amerigo, 33

Webb, Walter Prescott, 19–21, 61, 73, 84, 110, 128
With His Pistol in His Hand, 1, 9, 20, 56, 61, 70–72, 78–79, 81, 127–28; criticism of, 82–86, 89, 93, 110, 117–18
World War II, 56–58, 102, 124